Ben Howard's approach to cooking is simple. It only takes talent and imagination. Lucky for us he shares his and takes a straightforward look at culinary and financial considerations.

The result is this little confidence-building book that puts most already prepared foods in the realm of "no problem. I can do it myself." It's invaluable for speed and economy in the kitchen.

Olga Bier
Co-author: *Chef Wolfe's New American Turkey Cookbook* (Addison Wesley, Pub.)
Columnist: Pot Luck with Olga Bier

I really like this neat little book — these recipes sound fun to try. They would be quick and easy for someone like me to use, requiring only knowledge of how to operate a can-opener and blender; and I do want to try some of Ben's "prepared-ahead-of-time" mixes for cakes, brownies and other baked goodies. This is a very helpful book.

Margaret Bryant
Editor / Independent Homemaker

MAKE YOUR OWN MIXES
AND PREPARED FOODS

Fast . . . fun . . . easy ways to
cut the COST . . . the CALORIES*
. . . and the CRUD

BEN HOWARD

*well, sometimes

RAINBOW BOOKS, INC.

MAKE YOUR OWN MIXES and Prepared Foods
by Ben Howard
Cover and Interior Design by Marilyn Ratzlaff
Cover Photo by William H. Frank

Library of Congress Cataloging in Publication
Howard, Ben, 1923-
    Make your own mixes and prepared foods : fast—fun—easy
ways to cut the cost—the calories (well, sometimes) and the crud /
by Ben Howard.
        p.   cm.
    ISBN 1-56825-007-X : $14.95
    1. Food mixes.   2. Cookery (Natural foods)   I. Title.
    TX652.H663 1993
    641.5'5—dc20   93-11724
                                                    CIP

CONTENTS

FOR YOU

If you choose to take all of two minutes to shred a chunk of Cheddar cheese rather than pay *an additional $1.60 a pound* for the preshredded stuff . . . THIS BOOK IS FOR YOU!

If you buy what you presume to be is a package of commonplace croutons, then are affronted by discovering it contains water, corn syrup, ammonium sulfate, ammonium chloride, calcium sulfate, potassium bromate, calcium peroxide, azodicarbonamide, protease enzymes, monocalcium phosphate, and calcium propionate . . . THIS BOOK IS FOR YOU!

If you truly take pleasure in preparing food and feel personally rewarded when you concoct your very own spice mix, chicken casserole, or cake frosting . . . THIS BOOK IS FOR YOU!

ABOUT THAT TITLE

The Cost . . .

As a rule of thumb — grocerywise — anytime anyone does anything for you, it's going to cost you money! For example, you'd be paying *$16 an hour* for someone else to grate that aforementioned Cheddar cheese.

If you shell out $1.03 for a fancy printed-in-full-color envelope of beef gravy mix (whose prime ingredients are probably flour and salt), you're actually paying *$.59 per tablespoonful!*

In her book, *Cheaper & Better*, Nancy Birnes does a splendid job of spelling out to the penny what the Do-It-Yourselfer can save, from $.02 (Basic Tomato Sauce) to $46.06 (Champagne Cooler).

I have elected to eschew this detailed accounting because I believe the obvious fact that one is saving substantially is undoubtedly more important than the specific amount. Besides, prices continually change. What makes this book worthwhile is the assurance of saving money *combined* with the satisfaction of producing Mixes and Prepared Foods that are nutritious, with safe, familiar ingredients, and no unnecessary stabilizers, chemical additives, or expensive packaging.

. . . the Calories . . .

Frankly, the alliteration was too good to waste. Anyway, I qualified it by stating "sometimes". While virtually all the salad dressings are low in calories, other recipes are certainly not (Spiced Tea Mix, for example).

However, in creating these homemade Mixes and Prepared Foods, whenever possible, the lowest calorie alternatives have been used. Nonfat milk is called for, as is the minimum amount of sugar. And, in the entire book, the "C" Word (*Cream*) is specified only once!

. . . the Crud

If you too, are appalled by discovering the simplest grocery-shelf item may contain sodium citrate, tricalcium phosphate, artificial color, nitrates, and nitrites, take heart. The only chemicals you will purposely add in creating your own Mixes will be salt, baking soda, and baking powder.

Also, in all instances, the most healthful, nutritious ingredients are listed: margarine instead of cholesterol-laden butter; whole wheat flour instead of white; nonfat milk and nonfat cottage cheese, etc.

THE LAST WORD

Each of these recipes in this book are meant to be Easy . . . Fast . . . and Fun . . . to prepare.

That's why there are no recipes for making mayonnaise (too tricky) or yeast breads (not for the faint-o-heart), or home-canned goodies (calls for sterilized jars and hot-water baths).

With one exception (making your own "Cream" Cheese), your time spent at the stove or kitchen counter should be minimal. While several concoctions call for lengthy simmering, marinading, ripening, or flavor-melding, they can do that by themselves while you've got your feet up.

Lastly, making your own Mixes and Prepared Foods should provide satisfaction, a sense of accomplishment, and be fun to do, besides saving you money.

If *doing it yourself* isn't *fun*, then what's the point?

DEDICATION

As the Great American Novel somehow seems to have slipped through my word processor, this slight tome will have to provide the base upon which my dedications rest. It is therefore dedicated with apologies and devotion to those past: Jimmie James and sweet Nancy . . . and to those present: Ol' Ger, Ratgirl, and, yes, most especially Mouse, who helped clean up the scraps from that twice-mentioned Cheddar cheese.

WITH MORE THAN THANKS

. . . with appreciation and deep gratitude to Betsy Lampé who discovered me . . . to Peggy Bryant who covered over my mistakes . . . to Marilyn Ratzlaff who made me look good . . . to Betty Wright who sat me on her lap and told me everything would be okay . . . and, not the least . . . to all the other talented troops at Rainbow Books, Inc.

PANTRY STANDBYS

ALL-PURPOSE BISCUIT MIX

6 cups all-purpose flour, unbleached preferred
3 TBS. Baking Powder (see recipe)
1 TBS. salt
1-1/4 cups solid shortening,
 Butter Flavor Crisco preferred

Combine flour, Baking Powder, and salt in a large bowl. Cut in shortening with 2 knives or pastry blender until mixture resembles coarse corn meal. Store in a container with tight-fitting lid.

Hints and Helps

One is sometimes warned of the "short shelf life" of baking powder with the recommendation that it is safer to discard questionable powder and buy fresh rather than risk ending up with a "dead" mix. First, I've had baking powder stay bright-eyed and bushy-tailed for more than five years. Secondly, it's easy to determine whether baking powder is still active: Pour 1/3 cup of boiling water on 1 teaspoon baking powder. If it bubbles enthusiastically, you're still in business.

Variations

For a healthier mix with improved flavor and more interesting texture, make All-purpose Biscuit Mix with 3 cups of white flour and 3 cups of whole wheat flour. For Buttermilk All-purpose Biscuit Mix, add 9 tablespoons dry buttermilk powder to the basic mix; it makes an ideal mix for all recipes listed below.

BASIC BISCUITS

2 cups All-purpose Biscuit Mix
1/2 cup milk

Blend Biscuit Mix and liquid with fork until stiff. Turn onto lightly floured surface; sprinkle dough lightly with flour to coat and knead only 8 to 10 times. Be gentle; don't overdo. If you're tough, you'll have tough biscuits. Pat to 1/2-inch thickness. Cut with 2-inch floured cutter or cut with sharp knife into 2-inch squares. Place on ungreased baking sheet 1 inch apart. Bake in preheated 425° oven 10 to 12 minutes. Makes 9 to 12 biscuits.

Variations

Biscuit Fingers
After kneading Basic Biscuits, shape into rope 1/2 inch in diameter; cut into 4-inch lengths. Place on baking sheet and brush with melted shortening. Bake in preheated oven 425° oven 12 to 15 minutes. Makes about 18 fingers; no thumbs.

Cinnamon Fingers
After brushing melted shortening on Biscuit Fingers (above), sprinkle with Cinnamon Sugar (see recipe).

Filled Biscuits
After cutting Basic Biscuits, brush 1 biscuit with melted shortening, add 1 teaspoon of tuna or cooked meat. Brush outer rim with water, top with second biscuit, and pinch to seal. Bake as for Basic Biscuits.

BASIC MUFFINS

2 cups All-purpose Biscuit Mix
2 TBS. granulated sugar
1 egg
2/3 cup milk

Combine Biscuit Mix and sugar in large bowl. Beat egg in separate bowl and add milk; beat to blend. Combine dry and liquid ingredients. Fill greased muffin pans 2/3 full. Bake in preheated 400° oven 18 to 22 minutes. Makes 9 large muffins.

Hints and Helps
Save and store in the refrigerator the parchment paper used to wrap cubes of margarine or butter. Use whenever a greased pan is called for, then discard.

Variations
Upside-down Muffins
Prepare Basic Muffins, increasing milk to 1 cup. Into each greased muffin cup, place:
1 tsp. margarine
2 tsp. brown sugar
2 tsp. chopped nuts
Spoon muffin mixture on top, filling 2/3 full. Bake in preheated 400° oven 20 to 25 minutes. Makes 10 muffins.

Orange Muffins
Prepare Basic Muffins, stirring 1 tablespoon grated orange rind into dry mixture, and use 1/3 cup orange juice and 1/3 cup milk for the liquid. Proceed as for Basic Muffins.

DUMPLINGS

1 cup All-purpose Biscuit Mix
1/3 cup milk

Combine Biscuit Mix and milk. Drop gently by spoonfuls into simmering soup or stew. Cover and simmer 15 minutes.

EASY BREAKFAST PUFF

1 lb. bulk pork sausage, browned and drained
   OR cooked, crumbled bacon
   OR cooked, chopped ham
1 cup All-purpose Biscuit Mix
1 cup Cheddar cheese, shredded
1 tsp. dry mustard
1/2 tsp. oregano
6 eggs
2 cups milk

Combine cooked meat, Biscuit Mix, cheese, dry mustard, oregano. Beat eggs thoroughly, then add milk and beat again; combine with dry mixture. Pour into shallow, greased 2-quart casserole; sprinkle top with paprika (optional). Bake in preheated 350° oven for about 1 hour, or until knife inserted into center comes out clean. Makes 6 servings.

Hints and Helps

All ingredients can be mixed earlier and refrigerated in a covered bowl until ready to pour into casserole. For luncheon menu, substitute 1 pound browned, then drained, ground beef for breakfast meat.

FAST FRUIT COBBLER

4 cups peeled, sliced apples, peaches, or nectarines
1/2 cup granulated sugar
1 TBS. All-purpose Biscuit Mix PLUS 2/3 cup Mix
1/2 tsp. All-purpose Baking Spice (see recipe)
    OR 1/2 tsp. ground cinnamon
2 TBS. brown sugar, firmly packed
1/4 cup margarine or vegetable shortening,
    preferably Butter Flavor Crisco
2 TBS. milk

Combine fruit, granulated sugar, 1 tablespoon Biscuit Mix, 1/2 teaspoon spice in a bowl, then spoon into shallow, well-greased 1-quart casserole. Using same bowl, combine remaining 2/3 cup Biscuit Mix with brown sugar. Cut in shortening with 2 knives until mixture is size of small peas. Stir in milk until moistened. Drop by teaspoonfuls onto fruit mixture. Bake in preheated 400° oven for 30 minutes or until toothpick inserted into crust comes out clean. Let stand 5 minutes.

SHORTCAKE

2 cups All-purpose Biscuit Mix
2 TBS. granulated sugar
2 TBS. melted margarine or Butter Flavor Crisco
1/2 cup milk

Combine all ingredients. Knead gently only 8 to 10 times. Pat to 1/2-inch thickness. Cut with 2-inch floured cutter or cut into 2-inch squares. Place one inch apart on baking sheet. Bake in preheated 425° oven 10 to 12 minutes. Separate shortcake with fork and fill with sugared fruit; garnish with more fruit and whipped topping.

WAFFLES OR PANCAKES

1 cup All-purpose Biscuit Mix
1 egg
2/3 cup milk
1 TBS. cooking oil, safflower preferred
1 TBS. granulated sugar (optional)

Beat egg with fork; add milk and oil and beat again. Add dry ingredients and mix gently with a fork (there should be small lumps).

WAFFLES: Bake in preheated waffle iron until desired shade of brown.

PANCAKES: Bake on hot (390°) griddle until bubbly; turn and brown other side.

Hints and Helps

The thinner the batter, the crisper the waffles and thinner the pancakes. Vary the quantity of milk slightly to suit your own individual taste.

Variations

Stir into batter 1 cup cooked, crumbled bacon OR 1 cup cooked, crumbled bulk sausage. For Blueberry Pancakes, stir in 1 cup fresh or frozen (thawed and drained) blueberries.

BASIC COOKIE MIX

3 cups all-purpose white flour, preferably unbleached,
   OR part white and part whole wheat flour
1-1/2 cups granulated sugar
1 cup dark brown sugar, firmly packed
1 tsp. Baking Powder (see recipe)
1 tsp. baking soda
1/2 tsp. salt
1 cup solid shortening,
   Butter Flavor Crisco preferred

Combine all dry ingredients in large bowl. Cut in shortening with pastry blender until mixture resembles coarse meal. Store in container with tight-fitting lid. Makes approximately 8 cups.

Basic baking instructions for all recipes below:
Drop prepared cookie dough by teaspoonfuls, approximately 2 inches apart, on well-greased baking sheet. Bake in preheated 350° oven 12 to 15 minutes. Remove with spatula to cooling rack.

CHOCOLATE COOKIES

2 cups Basic Cookie Mix
1 egg, unbeaten
3 TBS. unsweetened cocoa
2 TBS. milk
1 tsp. Vanilla Extract (see recipe)

Combine all ingredients until well blended. Follow Basic Baking Instructions above. Makes approximately 40 cookies.

Variations

Add 1/2 cup chocolate chips OR 1/2 cup peanut butter chips and/or 1/2 cup raisins and/or 1/2 cup chopped nuts.

CHOCOLATE CHIP COOKIES

2 cups Basic Cookie Mix
1 egg, unbeaten
1 TBS. milk
1 tsp. Vanilla Extract (see recipe)
1 cup chocolate chips

Combine Basic Cookie Mix with egg, milk, and Vanilla Extract until well blended. Add chocolate chips and mix thoroughly. Follow Basic Baking Instructions above. Makes approximately 40 cookies.

Variations

Add 1/2 to 1 cup of uncooked, old-fashioned or quick-cooking rolled oats and/or 1/2 cup raisins and/ or 1/2 cup chopped nuts. Be creative!

GINGER COOKIES

Different again from Old-fashioned Ginger Snaps (see recipe).

2 cups Basic Cookie Mix
1 egg, unbeaten
1 TBS. dark molasses
4 tsp. ground ginger
1 tsp. ground cinnamon
1/4 tsp. baking soda

Combine all ingredients until well blended. Follow Basic Baking Instructions above. Because of molasses, these cookies tend to stick, so make certain cookie sheet is very well greased. Makes approximately 40 cookies.

MOLASSES COOKIES

2 cups Basic Cookie Mix
1 egg, unbeaten
1 TBS. dark molasses
1/2 tsp. ground cinnamon
1/2 tsp. ground cloves
1/4 tsp. baking soda

Combine all ingredients until well blended. Follow Basic Baking Instructions above. Because of molasses, these cookies tend to stick, so make certain cookie sheet is very well greased. Makes approximately 40 cookies.

OATMEAL COOKIES

2 cups Basic Cookie Mix
1/2 cup uncooked, old-fashioned or quick-cooking
    rolled oats
1/2 cup raisins
1/2 cup chopped nuts
1 egg, unbeaten
2 TBS. milk
1 tsp. All-purpose Baking Spice (see recipe)
    OR 1 tsp. ground cinnamon
1 tsp. Vanilla Extract (see recipe)

Combine all ingredients until well blended. Follow the Basic Baking Instructions above. Makes approximately 4-1/2 dozen cookies.

Variations

Substitute 1/2 cup chopped dates, dried figs, or mixed dried fruit for the raisins in the above recipe. For Chocolate Chip Oatmeal Cookies, increase oats to 1 cup, and substitute 1 cup of chocolate chips for the dried fruit and nuts. As stated previously: be creative!

OLD-FASHIONED SPICE COOKIES

2 cups Basic Cookie Mix
1 egg, unbeaten
1 TBS. dark molasses
2 tsp. All-purpose Baking Spice (see recipe)
   OR 1-1/2 tsp. ground cinnamon plus 1/2 tsp.
   ground nutmeg
   OR 1/2 tsp. ground allspice
1/4 tsp. ground cloves
2/3 cup raisins
1/4 tsp. baking soda

Combine all ingredients until well blended. Follow Basic Baking Instructions above. Makes approximately 40 cookies.

SUGAR COOKIES

2 cups Basic Cookie Mix
1 egg, unbeaten
1 TBS. milk
1 tsp. Vanilla Extract (see recipe)
Granulated sugar

Combine all ingredients until well blended. Refrigerate dough until well chilled, 1 hour or longer. Then, using your hands, roll dough into small balls (if sticky, lightly coat your palms with salad oil) and drop into a small bowl with granulated sugar, turning to coat. Place on cookie sheet and follow Basic Baking Instructions above. Makes approximately 40 cookies.

VANILLA COOKIES

2 cups Basic Cookie Mix
1 egg, unbeaten
2 tsp. milk
2 tsp. (or to taste) Vanilla Extract (see recipe)

Combine all ingredients until well blended. Follow Basic Baking Instructions above. Makes approximately 40 cookies.

BASIC CAKE MIX

6 cups all-purpose flour (sifted, then measured)
4-1/2 cups granulated sugar
3-3/4 tsp. baking soda
3 tsp. Baking Powder (see recipe)
9 TBS. (1/2 cup plus 1 TBS.) instant nonfat dry
  milk solids
2 cups vegetable shortening, preferably
  Butter Flavor Crisco

Sift flour, sugar, baking soda, and Baking Powder together in a large bowl; add dry milk solids and mix thoroughly. Cut in shortening with a pastry blender until the consistency of corn meal. Store mix in a container with a tight-fitting lid. Makes 14-1/2 cups, enough for 3 two-layer cakes or up to 72 cupcakes.

GOLDEN YELLOW CAKE

4-3/4 cups Basic Cake Mix (see recipe)
3/4 cup water
3 eggs, unbeaten
1 tsp. Vanilla Extract (see recipe)

With a fork, gently stir Basic Cake Mix in its container; measure 4-3/4 cups into a bowl and with a fork stir in water, Vanilla Extract, and eggs, one at a time. With an electric mixer at medium speed, mix for no more than 2 minutes. Pour into two 8-inch, well-greased, then floured layer pans. Bake in a preheated 350° oven 25 to 30 minutes, until edges begin to pull away from the pan. Cool the cake on a rack for 5 minutes, then remove from pan and cool on a rack; this will keep the crust dry and prevent it from becoming soggy.

If baking cupcakes, fill up to 24 greased and floured muffin cups 2/3 full − or use paper cup liners − and bake in preheated 375º oven 20 to 25 minutes.

Hints and Helps
Overbeating can make a cake too fine-grained and close, so combine the dry ingredients with liquids as quickly as possible by hand. Beat with the electric mixer only until ingredients are well blended.

MOCHA CAKE

Golden Yellow Cake recipe (see above)
1 TBS. unsweetened cocoa
2 tsp. instant coffee powder or crystals

Follow directions for preparing Golden Yellow Cake, adding the cocoa and instant coffee. Bake as specified above.

RICH CHOCOLATE CAKE

Golden Yellow Cake recipe (see above)
1/3 cup unsweetened cocoa

Follow directions for preparing Golden Yellow Cake, adding the cocoa. Bake as specified above.

SPICE CAKE

Golden Yellow Cake recipe (see above)
1-1/2 tsp. All-purpose Baking Spice (see recipe)
    OR 1 tsp. ground cinnamon, plus 1/4 tsp. ground
    nutmeg and 1/4 tsp. ground cloves

Follow directions for preparing Golden Yellow Cake, adding the ground spices. Bake as specified above.

BASIC FRUIT BAR MIX

4 cups all-purpose white flour,
   OR, preferably 2 cups white and 2 cups whole
   wheat flour
2 cups solid shortening,
   preferably Butter Flavor Crisco
1 cup granulated sugar
1 cup brown sugar, firmly packed
1 tsp. baking soda
1/2 tsp. salt

Combine all ingredients in a large bowl and mix with pastry blender until crumbly and well blended. Store in container with tight-fitting lid. Makes 9 cups Fruit Bar Mix, sufficient for 2 batches of any of the following Fruit Bar recipes.

Variation
   If you prefer Fruit Bars with a rolled oats crumb base, add 1 cup of uncooked, old-fashioned or quick-cooking oats when preparing any of the recipes below.

EASY FRUIT BARS

4-1/2 cups Basic Fruit Bar Mix
1 egg, slightly beaten*
1 tsp. Vanilla Extract (see recipe)
1-1/2 tsp. All-purpose Baking Spice (see recipe)
   OR 1 tsp. ground cinnamon AND 1/2 tsp. ground
   nutmeg

*Use 2 eggs, slightly beaten, if you have added 1 cup of rolled oats to your Basic Fruit Bar Mix.

Combine all ingredients with a fork. Spread approximately half the Fruit Bar mixture in a greased 8 x 8-inch pan. (Use a greased 9 x 9-inch pan if you have added 1 cup of rolled oats to your mix.) Press with a spatula or back of spoon to make a thin layer over entire bottom of baking pan. Sprinkle on 1 cup of your choice of fruits, nuts or chocolate, or any combination thereof (see below). Using a fork and your fingers, top with the remaining crumb mixture (it will spread to cover during baking). Bake in a preheated 350° oven 30 minutes. Cool and cut into squares. Makes up to 24 bars.

Fillings
Use a total of 1 cup of the following ingredients for each batch of bars:

Raisins, chopped dates, figs, prunes, shredded or flaked coconut, dried apricots or apples, well-drained crushed pineapple, walnuts, almonds, pecans, unsalted peanuts, coarsely chopped, chocolate, peanut butter, or butterscotch chips.

COMPANY'S COMIN' DATE BARS

4-1/2 cups Basic Fruit Bar Mix (see recipe)
1-1/2 cups chopped dates
1/3 cup granulated sugar
1/4 cup orange juice
1 tsp. dried Orange Peel (see recipe)
  OR grated peel of 1 orange
1/2 cup chopped walnuts or pecans

Prepare crumb crust for Easy Fruit Bars (see above) and spread half the mixture in a greased 8 x 8-inch pan (9 x 9-inch pan if adding rolled oats). Combine balance of ingredients, EXCEPT nuts, and cook, stirring occasionally, over low heat until mixture thickens. Cool slightly; stir in nuts and spread date/nut mixture over crumb crust base. Top with remaining crumb crust and bake according to Easy Fruit Bar instructions above.

FANCY RAISIN BARS

4-1/2 cups Basic Fruit Bar Mix (see recipe)
1-1/2 cups dark or light raisins
1/2 cup water
1/4 cup brown sugar, firmly packed
1 TBS. lemon juice
1 tsp. freshly grated lemon rind
1 tsp. cornstarch
1/2 tsp. ground ginger
1/4 tsp. salt

Prepare crumb crust for Easy Fruit Bars (see above) OMITTING the spices and spread half the mixture in a greased 8 x 8-inch pan. Coarsely chop raisins and combine with all remaining ingredients. Cook raisin mixture over low heat, stirring occasionally, until thickened, about 10 minutes. Cool slightly and spread over crumb crust base. Top with remaining crumb crust and bake according to Easy Fruit Bar instructions above.

HERMITS

2-1/2 cups Basic Fruit Bar Mix
1 egg, unbeaten
1/4 cup milk
1 cup raisins
1/2 cup uncooked, old-fashioned or quick-cooking
    rolled oats
1/2 cup nuts, chopped
2-1/2 tsp. All-purpose Baking Spice (see recipe)
    OR 1 tsp. ground cinnamon, 1 tsp. ground all-
    spice, and 1/2 tsp. ground cloves

Combine Basic Fruit Bar Mix with egg and milk; blend well. Add balance of ingredients. Drop by large teaspoonfuls, about 2 inches apart, on well-greased cookie sheet (or one coated with nonstick cooking spray). Bake in preheated 375° oven 12 minutes. Makes approximately 4-1/2 dozen cookies.

PUDDING MIXES

BUTTERSCOTCH PUDDING & PIE FILLING MIX

1-3/4 cups brown sugar, firmly packed
3/4 cup instant nonfat dry milk solids
1 cup cornstarch
1/4 tsp. salt

Combine all ingredients and store in container with tight-fitting lid. Makes 3 cups mix, sufficient for 24 individual servings of prepared pudding.

To prepare:
Stir mix in container before measuring. For each 2 servings, use 1/4 cup of Butterscotch Pudding Mix and 1 cup of milk. Combine mix and milk in small saucepan with 2 tablespoons margarine and heat over very low flame, stirring constantly, until mixture boils. Boil gently, stirring, for 1 minute. Remove from heat and pour into 2 individual serving dishes. Refrigerate; pudding will thicken further as it chills.

CHOCOLATE PUDDING & PIE FILLING MIX

2 cups granulated sugar
1 cup unsweetened cocoa
2/3 cup cornstarch

Combine all ingredients and store in container with tight-fitting lid. Makes 3 cups mix, sufficient for 12 individual servings of prepared pudding.

To prepare:
For each 1/2 cup of Chocolate Pudding Mix, use 1-1/3 cups of milk. Combine mix, milk, and 4 teaspoons margarine in small saucepan, and heat over very low flame, stirring constantly, until mixture boils. Boil gently, stirring, for 1 minute. Pour into 2 individual serving dishes. Refrigerate.

Variations
Add 1/4 to 1/2 teaspoon mint extract after removing from heat. OR, add 1 tablespoon instant coffee powder or crystals before cooking. Also, 1/2 cup of chopped nuts can be added before pouring into serving dishes.

COCONUT CREAM PUDDING & PIE FILLING MIX

1-1/2 cups instant nonfat dry milk solids
1 cup granulated sugar
1 cup cornstarch
1/2 cup shredded coconut
1/2 tsp. salt

Combine all ingredients, except coconut, until well blended. Pulverize the coconut in blender; add to the dry mixture. Store in container with tight-fitting lid. Makes approximately 3-1/3 cups, sufficient for 24 individual servings of prepared pudding.

To prepare:
Stir mix in container before measuring. For each 2 servings, use 2/3 cup of Coconut Cream Pudding Mix and 1 cup of milk. Combine mix and milk in small saucepan, and heat over very low flame, stirring constantly, until mixture boils. Boil gently, stirring, for 1 minute. Remove from heat and stir in 1 teaspoon liquid coconut extract. Pour into 2 individual serving dishes. Refrigerate; pudding will thicken further as it chills.

VANILLA PUDDING MIX

1-1/2 cups instant nonfat dry milk solids
1 cup granulated sugar
1 cup cornstarch
1/2 tsp. salt

Combine all ingredients and store in container with tight-fitting lid. Makes 3 cups mix, sufficient for 24 individual servings of prepared pudding.

To prepare:
Stir mix in container before measuring. For each 2 servings, use 1/4 cup of Vanilla Pudding Mix and 1 cup of milk. Combine mix, milk, and 1 tablespoon margarine in small saucepan, and heat over very low flame, stirring constantly, until mixture boils. Boil gently, stirring, for 1 minute. Remove from heat and stir in 1/2 teaspoon Vanilla Extract (see recipe) or to taste. Pour into 2 individual serving dishes. Refrigerate; pudding will thicken further as it chills.

Variations
Before preparing, add 1/2 teaspoon ground nutmeg OR 1/2 teaspoon All-purpose Baking Spice (see recipe) to each 1/4 cup of Vanilla Pudding Mix. OR, for liquid, use 1/4 cup Maple Syrup (see recipe) and 3/4 cup of milk; reduce Vanilla Extract to 1/4 teaspoon.

SHAKE 'N BAKE

1/2 cup all-purpose flour
1/2 cup fine dry bread crumbs,
   OR crushed corn flake crumbs,
   OR crushed cracker crumbs,
   OR any combination thereof
2 TBS. cornstarch
2 tsp. granulated sugar
2 tsp. chicken bouillon granules
2 tsp. Poultry Seasoning (see recipe)
2 tsp. paprika
1 tsp. salt (or to taste)
1 tsp. onion powder
1/2 tsp. garlic powder

Combine all ingredients and store in container with tight-fitting lid.

Chicken
Coat with salad oil. Spoon several tablespoons of mix into paper grocery bag. Place 2 pieces of chicken at a time in bag and shake well to coat. Bake on a shallow, well-greased pan (or coat liberally with nonstick cooking spray) in preheated 425° over 20 minutes. Turn and bake 20 minutes more.

Hints and Helps
The easiest way to coat chicken is to dump all the pieces in a plastic grocery bag; pour in about 1 tablespoon oil. Twist bag top to close, then massage the chicken pieces in the bag until well coated.

If you prefer, you can eliminate coating with oil. Instead, dip pieces of chicken in a mixture of 1 beaten egg to 1/2 cup milk; then drop individual pieces of chicken in the paper bag with mix and shake lightly to coat. Let pieces dry completely before placing in the baking pan. Proceed as above.

Fish

Brush with oil or melted margarine. Place several tablespoons of mix in a shallow bowl; dip in fish and pat to coat. Bake on shallow, well-greased pan (or coat liberally with nonstick cooking spray) in preheated 375° oven 10 minutes. Turn and bake 10 minutes more.

Pork Chops

Prepare as with fish, and bake in preheated 425° oven for 20 minutes. Turn and bake 15 minutes more.

NO-GUESS PIE CRUST MIX

7 cups all-purpose flour, unbleached preferred
3 cups solid vegetable shortening,
   Butter Flavor Crisco preferred
1 tsp. salt

Sift flour onto a large sheet of waxed paper; measure out 7 cups, add salt, and sift again into a large bowl. Add solid shortening by spoonfuls and cut it into the flour mixture with 2 crisscross knives until mixture is crumbly and coarse, with largest lumps the size of small peas. Store in a cool place in container with tight-fitting lid. Makes approximately 11 cups of mix.

To prepare crust, place 1/2 cup of all-purpose flour in a small bowl, and blend in 6 tablespoons cold water. Spoon 2-3/4 cups of Pie Crust Mix into a bowl, and add the flour/water mixture by dollops, blending in lightly with a fork until mixture sticks together. If necessary, work the dough gently with your hands until it can be gathered into a ball. Turn dough onto floured surface and with floured rolling pin gently roll out dough, proceeding as with any pie crust.

This recipe makes a very generous crust for the largest size pie pan and allows for both top and bottom crust. For an 8-inch pie pan, use 2 cups Pie Crust Mix and add a flour/water mixture of 1/3 cup flour to 4 tablespoons water.

Hints and Helps
The secret of good pie crust is "keep the air in and the moisture out." This is why *2 siftings* are suggested and why *crisscross knives*, rather than a pastry blender, are recommended.

Don't throw away any leftover pie crust dough. Simply roll it out into small circles, add a dollop of jam to the center of each circle, fold over top, seal edges, cut small air vent in top, and bake along with your pie. These quick tarts will bake in less than half the time of the pie.

BETTY BELL'S FRUIT CRISP MIX

This Crisp has all the qualities of pie crust, without the need to roll it out and make top and bottom crusts.

> 3 cups all-purpose flour
>   OR, preferably, half white and
>   half whole wheat flour
> 4 cups sugar, either all granulated
>   OR, preferably, half granulated and
>   half brown sugar
> 1-1/3 cups solid vegetable shortening,
>   Butter Flavor Crisco preferred

Combine flour and sugar; mix in shortening with pastry blender until the consistency of corn meal. Store in container with tight-fitting lid. Makes approximately 10 cups, sufficient for 4 Crisps.

To prepare Apple Crisp:

> 4 cups tart apples, pared and sliced or diced
> 1 TBS. lemon juice, fresh or bottled
> 1 tsp. All-purpose Baking Spice (see recipe)
>   OR 1 tsp. ground cinnamon

Combine apples, lemon juice, and spice with 3 tablespoons water and place in a greased 8 x 8-inch or 10 x 6-inch pan. Measure approximately 2-1/2 cups of Crisp Mix and sprinkle over top. Bake in preheated 350° oven for 40 minutes or until top is very lightly browned. Serve at room temperature. Top with frozen yogurt or ice cream, if desired.

Variations

Instead of apples, substitute fresh or canned peaches (use 3 tablespoons canned juice instead of water), apricots, or nectarines. If using blackberries, raspberries, blueberries, or plums, omit the water and mix fruit with 2 tablespoons quick-cooking tapioca.

BRAN MUFFIN MIX

3 cups bran
2-1/2 cups all-purpose flour
  OR half white and half whole wheat flour
1/3 cup buttermilk powder
1-1/2 cups granulated sugar
  OR 1/1-2 cups low calorie sugar replacement
2-1/2 tsp. baking soda

Combine all ingredients well and store in container with tight-fitting lid. Makes 6 cups mix.

To prepare:

2 cups Bran Muffin Mix
1 cup water
2 TBS. cooking oil, safflower oil preferred
1 egg, unbeaten

Combine Bran Muffin Mix with water in mixing bowl; let stand 5 minutes. Add oil and egg and mix well. Fill well-greased muffin cups 3/4 full. Bake in pre-heated 400° oven for 20 to 25 minutes or until tops are very lightly browned and spring back when touched. Makes 9 muffins.

Hints and Helps

This recipe works best in well-greased muffin pans or those sprayed with nonstick cooking spray. Paper muffin cups are NOT recommended as muffins stick badly to the paper unless chilled overnight in the refrigerator after baking.

Variations

Add 2 teaspoons All-purpose Baking Spice (see recipe) to prepared Bran Muffin Mix. Add 1/2 cup of any of the following to prepared Bran Muffin Mix: chopped, pared apples; chopped dates; raisins. Makes 12 muffins.

CHOCOLATE BROWNIE MIX

3-3/4 cups granulated sugar
2-1/3 cups all-purpose flour
1-1/3 cups unsweetened cocoa
1 tsp. Baking Powder
1 tsp. salt
2 cups solid shortening,
   Butter Flavor Crisco preferred

Combine dry ingredients and cut in shortening with pastry blender until mixture resembles corn meal (it may be moist and somewhat gummy). Store in container with tight-fitting lid. Makes approximately 10 cups, sufficient for 4 pans of Brownies.

To prepare chewy Chocolate Brownies:

2 eggs, unbeaten
1 tsp. Vanilla Extract (see recipe)
1/2 cup chopped nuts

Measure approximately 2-1/2 cups Chocolate Brownie Mix into a bowl. Mix in eggs and Vanilla Extract (mixture will be somewhat grainy). Add nuts and mix well (mixture will become smooth). Spread evenly in 8 x 8-inch, greased pan. Bake in preheated 350° oven for 20 minutes. Center should appear slightly underdone; for more cake-like Brownies, bake an additional 5 minutes.

Variations

Substitute 1/2 cup peanut butter chips for nuts OR add 1/2 cup of raisins OR 1/2 cup of chopped dates OR 1/2 cup shredded coconut OR 1/2 cup of chocolate chips to basic Chocolate Brownies.

NOODLES

EGG NOODLES

2/3 cup all-purpose flour, preferably unbleached
1 egg
1/2 tsp. salt

Beat egg slightly with salt and mix in flour to make a rather stiff dough. Knead on floured surface briefly, then let rest, covered, for 1/2 hour. On floured surface, with rolling pin, roll dough until it is very thin. Let dry, uncovered, until it loses all stickiness, but is not dry or brittle. Fold it over several times and cut into narrow strips. Separate strips with your fingers and let noodles dry thoroughly. Store in closed container for future use or use immediately.

To cook: Drop in boiling salted water or stock and boil gently for 5 minutes. Drain at once. Add a dollop of margarine and stir gently to prevent cooked noodles from sticking together.

Variation
For a healthier combination, a slightly different flavor, and a more interesting texture, use approximately half white and half whole wheat flour.

CHINESE CRISP NOODLES

These noodles can be made fresh (directions below) or by deep frying leftover thin spaghetti or noodles. Just pour boiling water over cold pasta to soften and separate, then drain thoroughly and fry according to the following directions.

Vermicelli or thin spaghetti or noodles
Salt

Boil noodles according to package directions, until just tender. Place in colander and rinse with cold water. Drain thoroughly. Fry them in deep fat fryer (385°-395°) until lightly browned. Drain on paper towel and sprinkle lightly with salt. Keep them hot in a low oven (250°) or, when thoroughly cooled, store in covered container. To reheat, place them in a 300° oven for a few minutes.

CORN MEAL NOODLES

Because of the increased amount of liquid, Corn Meal Noodles take much longer to dry than regular noodles. Make sure you allow plenty of drying time before cooking or storing.

>1 cup corn meal, yellow or white
>1 TBS. margarine
>1-1/2 cups boiling water
>1 egg, beaten
>1/2 cup all-purpose flour
>1-1/2 tsp. Baking Powder (see recipe)
>1/2 tsp. salt OR Seasoned Salt (see recipe)

Melt margarine in boiling water, pour in corn meal and remove from heat. Mix with a fork until well blended. Cool slightly and mix in beaten egg. Sift together the flour, Baking Powder, and salt; add to cornmeal mixture, blending well. With floured hands, form dough into 4 equal-sized balls and let rest on well-floured surface, covered with cloth or paper towels, for 1/2 hour. Roll each ball as thin as possible on well-floured surface (pastry cloth works best) with floured rolling pin. Cut into narrow strips with sharp knife and gently scatter on ungreased cookie sheets in a single layer. Warm in a 200° oven until thoroughly dry. Cook immediately or store in closed container for future use.

To cook: Drop into boiling salted water or stock and simmer gently for 5 minutes. Drain at once. Add a dollop of margarine and stir gently to prevent cooked noodles from sticking together.

Hints and Helps

On a warm day, Corn Meal Noodles can be air-dried on cloth or paper towels. Whether using air or oven drying method, do not layer individual noodle strips as they tend to flatten and stick together.

GREEN NOODLES

1/4 cup puréed cooked spinach
1 egg, beaten
1/4 tsp. salt
2 cups all-purpose flour

Combine spinach, egg, and salt in a bowl. Gradually stir in flour and then knead, on floured surface, until smooth. Cover and let rest for 1/2 hour. Proceed as with Egg Noodles, above.

HEALTH BARS

These fruit-topped Health Bars require a lot of ingredients, but the results are worth it. You'll feel enriched and invigorated with each bite.

Fruit Topping
    1-1/3 cups snipped mixed dried fruit
      (use packaged mixed fruit and/or raisins, dates, figs, prunes, etc.)
    2 TBS. solid or liquid shortening,
      Butter Flavor Crisco or safflower oil preferred
    1 egg, slightly beaten
    1 cup chopped nuts OR Grape Nuts cereal
    1/2 cup brown sugar, packed
    1/2 cup whole wheat flour
    4 TBS. wheat bran
    4 TBS. toasted wheat germ
    1-1/4 tsp. ground cinnamon
    1/2 tsp. ground nutmeg
      OR ground allspice OR ground cloves
    1 tsp. salt

Combine snipped fruit, shortening, and 2/3 cup *boiling* water; let stand for 5 minutes. Add balance of ingredients and combine. Set aside to spread over crust.

Crust
    4 TBS. solid or liquid shortening,
      Butter Flavor Crisco or safflower oil preferred
    4 TBS. brown sugar
    2 TBS. honey or light corn syrup
    2 TBS. molasses
    1 egg, slightly beaten
    2 cups uncooked, old-fashioned or quick-cooking rolled oats
    4 TBS. whole wheat flour

Mix shortening, sugar, honey, molasses, and egg together, then add oats and flour until well combined. Using a fork, press into 13 x 9 x 2-inch baking pan which is *well greased* or coated with nonstick cooking spray. Bake in preheated 350° oven for 5 minutes.

Remove from oven, spread fruit mixture evenly over crust and bake an additional 25 to 30 minutes. When cooled completely, cut into bars.

NO-BAKE HEALTH BARS

1-1/2 cups chunky peanut butter
1 cup honey
3/4 cup brown sugar
3 cups uncooked, old-fashioned, or quick-cooking
   rolled oats
2 cups bran or bran cereal
1 cup snipped packaged dried fruit
   OR snipped dates and/or prunes and/or raisins

Combine peanut butter, honey, and brown sugar in a large saucepan; bring just to a boil, stirring constantly to blend. Immediately remove from heat, stir in oats, bran, and snipped fruit. Spray 13 x 9 x 2-inch pan with nonstick cooking spray and press mixture evenly into pan, using spatula sprayed with nonfat cooking spray, or by covering mixture with waxed paper and pressing firmly with your hands. Cool thoroughly before cutting into bars.

GRANOLA

6 cups uncooked, old-fashioned, or quick-cooking
   rolled oats
1 cup wheat germ
1 cup chopped, mixed nuts
1 cup snipped mixed dried fruit (use packaged
   mixed dried fruit) and/or raisins, dates, figs,
   prunes, etc.
1 cup sunflower OR sesame OR pumpkin seeds,
   preferably a combination of all three.
1/2 cup wheat bran
1/2 cup shredded coconut
1/2 cup cooking oil, safflower oil preferred
1/2 cup honey
1/4 cup molasses
1 TBS. Vanilla Extract (see recipe)
2 tsp. ground cinnamon
1 tsp. ground nutmeg OR ground allspice
   OR ground cloves

Thoroughly combine all ingredients. Bake in an
ungreased 13 x 9 x 2-inch pan in a preheated 350° oven
20 to 25 minutes, stirring frequently to brown lightly
and evenly. Cool. Stir until crumbly. Store in a container with tight-fitting lid.

OLD BEN'S GRANOLA BARS

1 cup Granola (see recipe)
1 cup uncooked, old-fashioned, or quick-cooking
   rolled oats
2/3 cup whole wheat flour
2/3 chopped nuts OR Grape Nuts cereal
2/3 cup chocolate chips
2/3 cup wheat germ OR wheat bran
1/4 cup brown sugar, packed
2 eggs, slightly beaten
1/2 cup honey OR light corn syrup OR half molasses and half honey or light corn syrup
1/4 cup cooking oil, safflower oil preferred
1 tsp. Vanilla Extract (see recipe)

Combine dry ingredients. Add eggs, honey, oil and
Vanilla Extract, stirring until well coated. Press evenly
into a 13 x 9 x 2-inch baking pan which has been
greased or coated with nonstick cooking spray. Bake in
preheated 325° oven 30 to 35 minutes or until lightly
browned around the edges and no longer sticky. When
cool, cut into bars.

BEER BREAD MIX

This Beer Bread Mix will serve two worthwhile purposes, besides being easy and fun to make: (1) If you're out of bread, you can make a most passable loaf of honest-to-gosh bread in less than an hour and a half. (2) If you're not already a bread baker, it may well give you the confidence to tackle yeast-baked breads.

> 3 cups all-purpose flour OR half white and half whole wheat flour OR 1-1/2 cups white, 1 cup whole wheat, 1/2 cup rye flour
> 4-1/2 tsp. Baking Powder (see recipe)
> 3 TBS. granulated sugar
> 1-1/2 tsp. salt

Combine all ingredients well and store in a covered container.

Hints and Helps

This mix is sufficient for 1 large or 2 small loaves. Double or triple the recipe if desired for future use, storing in covered container. Measure out 3 cups plus 4 tablespoons of Beer Bread Mix for each batch of bread.

To prepare:

> 1 Beer Bread Mix recipe
> 1 12-ounce can beer, dark or light, but not "lite"

Preheat oven and grease loaf pan(s). Combine Beer Bread Mix and beer and bake as follows:

> 1 large loaf - 350° for 1-1/4 hours
> 2 small loaves - 400° for 45 minutes

CHEDDAR SNACK CRACKERS

There's no comparison between "boughten" Cheddar crackers and these crisp delicacies: they're addictive! To spread anything on them would be an insult.

> 3/4 cup all-purpose white flour OR equal parts
>   white and whole wheat flour
> 1/4 cup wheat germ
> 1 tsp. oregano
> 1/2 tsp. dry mustard
> 1/4 tsp. Seasoned Salt (see recipe) or salt
> 1/3 cup softened margarine or Butter Flavor Crisco
> 1-1/2 cups finely shredded Cheddar cheese
> 2 TBS. sesame seeds
> 1 TBS. minced dried onion
> 2 TBS. milk

In a small dish, combine dried minced onion with milk and set aside. Combine flour, wheat germ, oregano, mustard, and salt, stirring to blend. Cut in shortening with pastry blender until well mixed. Add cheese, sesame seeds, and onion/milk mixture. With your hands, shape into 2 firm rolls about 1-1/2 inches in diameter. Wrap in plastic wrap, foil, or waxed paper and refrigerate several hours or overnight, until thoroughly chilled. Slice with sharp knife into thin wafers 1/8 to 1/4 inches thick. Place on greased baking sheet; bake in preheated 350° oven for 12 to 14 minutes or until lightly browned. Cool immediately on cake rack. Store in covered container. Makes between 40 to 60 crackers, depending upon how thick they were cut.

Hints and Helps
1/4 cup of finely minced scallions or onion can be substituted for the dried minced onion, in which case add only enough milk (up to 2 tablespoons) to hold mixture together.

JIMMIE JAMES' CORN MEAL CRACKERS

The secret of these crispy critters is to get them paper-thin, which, with a little practice, is easy.

> 1 cup corn meal, yellow or white
> 1 tsp. Seasoned Salt (see recipe)
> 1 tsp. onion powder
> 1 tsp. celery seed, slightly crushed
> 1/4 tsp. ground pepper
> 1 TBS. Parmesan cheese
> 1 cup boiling water
> 3 TBS. melted bacon fat (preferred) or margarine

Mix corn meal and all dry ingredients in a bowl. Add boiling water and blend well. Stir in melted bacon fat or margarine. Drop small quantities from tip of teaspoon onto greased baking sheet. Using a knife blade or small spatula dipped into ice water, then wiped with a paper towel, flatten each wafer until very thin, about 1/16 inch. Bake in preheated 350° oven 15 minutes or until toasty brown. Cool on cake rake and store in covered container. Makes about 60 2-inch crackers.

Variation

Substitute 1/2 teaspoon (or more to taste) chili powder for the ground pepper.

HEALTHY CROUTONS

Most packaged croutons are too greasy, too salty, and too pale. Make your own and make them the way you like them!

Buy a loaf of "mooshy" store-bought bread, preferably whole wheat. If time permits, unwrap it and "shingle" the slices on a large cookie sheet, or in a large bowl, and let sit overnight. Dice the bread into approximately 3/4-inch squares, leaving the crusts on. (If you wish to use a small amount of fat, melt a dollop of bacon fat, or margarine, on a large cookie sheet with rim in a 325° oven just until fat is melted.) Scatter diced bread cubes on the cookie sheet and bake in the oven until as brown as you like, turning cubes about every 10 minutes, until all cubes become evenly brown.

Remove cookie sheet from oven and dump browned cubes into a large paper shopping bag. Add your choice of seasonings (see below) and carefully rotate the bag to coat. When thoroughly cooled, store in a large covered container.

Seasonings
One teaspoon or more (to taste) of each or any combination of the following:
Onion powder
Garlic powder
Herb of your choice, such as thyme, marjoram, oregano, savory, ground rosemary
Salad herbs (see recipe)
Poultry Seasoning (see recipe)
Parmesan cheese (at least 1 or 2 TBS.)

TORTILLA CHIPS

Perhaps fortunately, perhaps unfortunately, once you've tried your own Tortilla Chips, you'll never go back to the packaged kind.

Corn or flour tortillas
Cooking oil, safflower oil preferred

Cut tortillas into eighths or into strips. Fill a deep-fat fryer or small iron skillet half full of oil. Heat to 350°, then drop the tortilla pieces, individually and quickly, into the fat. Cook until they are as brown as you like. (If using a frying pan, you may wish to turn them over after about a half minute.) Drain on paper towels and salt immediately. Cool thoroughly before storing in a container with tight-fitting lid.

Variation
When cooling, sprinkle lightly with a combination of 1/2 salt and 1/2 chili powder.

MELBA TOAST

French bread baguette,
  OR rye baguette,
  OR similar firm bread

Slice bread as thinly as possible: 1/8 to 3/16 inches. Place the bread flat on an ungreased cookie sheet and bake in a 300° oven until it becomes crisp and slightly browned, turning once or twice if necessary. Remove from oven and when cool, place in container with tight-fitting lid.

ONION SOUP MIX

Why? Why pay almost 75¢ for a foil-lined envelope, a box, and 1.1 ounces of "beefy" onion soup mix when for pennies you can make your own? Incidentally, the packaged kind also includes cornstarch and flour with nary a mention of "beef."

>   1 TBS. minced dried onion
>   1 tsp. beef bouillon granules
>   Dash of ground pepper
>   Dash of paprika

Combine all ingredients in a small saucepan. Add 1 cup (8 ounces) of water and simmer for 8 minutes. Makes 1 serving. Recipe can easily be doubled, tripled, etc.

Hints and Helps

If you ordinarily cook for two or more, it is convenient to make this Onion Soup Mix in the larger quantities you will need and store in carefully sealed small plastic bags.

ONION SOUP CHIP DIP

Dry ingredients for 1 serving Onion Soup Mix (see
    recipe)
1 pt. (16 oz.) sour cream, nonfat or sour cream
    substitute preferred

Blend dry ingredients and sour cream thoroughly
and chill for several hours to bring out the flavor.

Variations

Substitute chicken bouillon granules for beef. If
desired, instead of sour cream, use one 8-oz. package of
reduced-calorie cream cheese and thin with milk to
desired dipping consistency. Also, try adding 1 tablespoon of sherry.

GOOD 'N DARK BROWN GRAVY MIX

Face it! Nothing makes good old-fashioned gravy like the drippings in a crusty brown roasting pan. However, here is a most satisfactory, quick gravy mix you can call upon "in a minute" to do justice to your mashed potatoes or noodles. Moreover, you aren't paying more than $1.00 for less than one ounce (!) of the packaged stuff.

    1-1/3 cups cornstarch
    5 TBS. + 1 tsp. beef bouillon granules
    4 tsp. instant coffee powder or crystals
    4 tsp. unsweetened cocoa
    2 tsp. onion powder
    1 tsp. garlic powder
    1/2 tsp. ground pepper
    1/2 tsp. paprika

Combine all ingredients and store in a container with tight-fitting lid. Sufficient for making 8 batches of gravy, 1-1/2 cups each.

To prepare:
Measure 3 tablespoons Brown Gravy Mix into a small saucepan. Add 1-1/2 cups water and bring to a boil, stirring constantly. Simmer, stirring for 1 minute.

Hints and Helps
The above recipe makes a low-calorie gravy; for richer gravy, add 2 tablespoons drippings saved from a cooked roast, bacon drippings, or margarine. Also add 1 teaspoon Bovril, Kitchen Bouquet, or Gravy Master, if desired.

UNCLE BENNIE'S WHITE SAUCE MIX

This makes foolproof, lump-free, rich, medium-thick white sauce that is also a base for countless other quick sauces (see below).

> 1-1/2 cups instant nonfat dry milk solids
> 1 cup all-purpose flour
> 1 cup Butter Flavor Crisco
> 1 tsp. salt
> 1/2 tsp. ground pepper
> 1/2 tsp. paprika

Blend the dry ingredients and cut in the Butter Flavor Crisco with a pastry blender until mixture resembles moist cornmeal. Store in container with tight-fitting lid. Makes approximately 4 cups coarse mix, sufficient for eight 1-cup portions of White Sauce.

To prepare:
For each 1-cup portion of White Sauce, measure 1/2 cup mix into saucepan. Add 1 cup milk and bring to a boil over low heat, stirring constantly. Boil gently for 1 minute.

Variation
White Sauce Mix can also be prepared using margarine instead of Butter Flavor Crisco. If so, store in the refrigerator in container with tight-fitting lid.

BÉCHAMEL SAUCE

Prepare White Sauce, above, but use half milk and half meat or vegetable stock for the liquid.

CHEESE SAUCE

Prepare White Sauce, above, but use only 3/4 cup of milk for the liquid. When smooth and gently boiling, add 1/2 cup or more of grated or diced cheese. Cook, stirring, until cheese melts.

CURRY SAUCE

Prepare White Sauce, above, adding 1 teaspoon Curry Powder (see recipe) or more, to taste, to dry mixture prior to cooking.

HORSERADISH SAUCE

Prepare White Sauce, above. After removing from heat, stir in 3 tablespoons prepared horseradish.

MUSTARD SAUCE

Prepare White Sauce, above, adding 1 teaspoon Prepared Hot Mustard (see recipe) to mixture prior to cooking.

VELOUTÉ SAUCE

Prepare White Sauce, above, but use meat or vegetable stock for the liquid.

SYRUPS

PANCAKE SYRUP

2 cups brown sugar, firmly packed
1/4 cup water

Combine brown sugar and water in saucepan. Heat until sugar dissolves completely. Store in container with tight-fitting lid.

MAPLE SYRUP

1-1/2 cups light corn syrup
1/4 cup brown sugar, firmly packed
2 TBS. water
3/4 tsp. maple syrup extract
3/4 tsp. Vanilla Extract (see recipe)

Combine corn syrup, brown sugar, and water; bring to boil and simmer, stirring constantly, for 2 minutes. Cool slightly; add maple syrup extract and Vanilla Extract. Store in container with tight-fitting lid.

NO-COOK PANCAKE SYRUP

3/4 cup honey
1/2 cup molasses
2 TBS. water
1 tsp. Vanilla Extract (see recipe)

Combine all ingredients in a small bowl and whisk until smooth (or use a blender). Store in container with tight-fitting lid.

FIG NEWTONS

Your own Fig Newtons won't come out as "precision cut" as the brand of renown, but they will have a fresh quality and tenderness that is most pleasing! Besides, You Did It Your Way.

Filling:

      1-1/2 cups dried figs, chopped
      3/4 cup water
      1/2 cup granulated sugar
      Juice of 1 lemon, or 2 TBS. bottled lemon juice

In a saucepan, combine all ingredients and cook over medium heat, stirring occasionally, then constantly as mixture thickens and becomes like jam. Cool.

Crust:

      1 cup brown sugar, firmly packed
      1/2 cup solid shortening,
         preferably Butter Flavor Crisco
      2 eggs, unbeaten
      1 tsp. Vanilla Extract (see recipe)
      2-1/2 cups all-purpose flour
      1/2 tsp. salt
      1/4 tsp. baking soda

In a bowl, cream sugar, shortening, eggs, and Vanilla Extract; stir in flour, salt, and soda. (For easier handling, chill dough if time permits.) Divide dough into 4 oblong rolls; place rolls, one at a time, on a floured surface (a pastry cloth is ideal). Using a floured rolling pin, roll dough to about 3-1/2 inches wide by 12 inches long.

Mound a small amount of the filling down the center of each strip; turn up the edges with a spatula to enclose the filling and press edges together lightly to seal. With a sharp knife, greased, and repeatedly dipped in flour, cut each strip into 10 pieces. Place, seam side

down, on a greased baking sheet and bake in a preheated 375° oven 10 to 12 minutes until very slightly
puffed and firm to the touch. Cool on a rack. Makes 40
Fig Newtons.

Variations

Any dried fruit, such as apples, raisins, peaches,
apricots, etc., or a medley of these fruits can be substituted for the figs. Mincemeat or thick jam can also be
used right from the jar, instead of the dried fruit/
sugar/water filling.

GINGER SNAPS

If you like the sharp taste of packaged Ginger Snaps, you'll find that these match them in zip, but have a lightness to boot.

> 2 cups all-purpose flour
> 1 TBS. ground ginger
> 2 tsp. ground cinnamon
> 2 tsp. baking soda
> 1/2 tsp. salt
> 3/4 cup solid shortening,
>   Butter Flavor Crisco preferred
> 1 cup granulated sugar
> 1 egg, unbeaten
> 1/4 cup dark molasses
> Granulated sugar

Combine flour, ginger, cinnamon, soda, and salt thoroughly in small bowl and set aside. Cream shortening and add sugar gradually until well blended. Beat in egg and molasses. Place flour mixture in sifter and sift over creamed mixture a little at a time, blending well after each addition. Form *small* teaspoons of dough into balls (about the size of a medium olive) by rolling them lightly, one at a time, between the palms of your hands. Roll dough balls in granulated sugar to coat entirely. Place 2 inches apart on ungreased baking sheet and bake in preheated 350° oven for 12 to 15 minutes, until tops are crackly, slightly rounded, and very lightly browned. Cool on rack and store in container with tight-fitting lid. Makes about 4 dozen cookies.

Hints and Helps
Forming dough balls in much easier if dough is chilled. Otherwise, grease palms lightly with salad oil to prevent dough from sticking to hands. When baking, watch carefully as bottoms can scorch easily.

PEANUT BUTTER COOKIES

1-1/4 cups all-purpose flour
3/4 tsp. baking soda
1/4 tsp. salt
1/2 cup peanut butter, creamy or chunky
1/2 cup solid shortening,
   Butter Flavor Crisco preferred
1/2 cup granulated sugar
1/2 cup brown sugar
1 egg, unbeaten
1/2 tsp. Vanilla Extract (see recipe)
Granulated sugar
Peanut halves (optional)

Sift flour, soda, and salt together and set aside. Thoroughly cream shortening, peanut butter, sugars, egg, and Vanilla Extract. Blend in flour mixture. Using palms of hands, shape into 1-inch balls. Roll dough balls in granulated sugar to coat entirely. Place 2 inches apart on ungreased cookie sheet. Press 4 or 5 peanut halves atop each cookie or make a crisscross pattern with fork tines. Bake in preheated 350° oven for 10 to 12 minutes. Cool on rack and store in tightly covered container. Makes about 4 dozen cookies.

SCHNOCKLES

CRACKER JACK

2 qts. popped corn, white or yellow
1 cup roasted peanuts, salted or unsalted
1/2 cup brown sugar, firmly packed
1/4 cup (1/2 stick) margarine
1/4 cup light or dark corn syrup
1/2 tsp. salt (ONLY if using unsalted peanuts)
1/4 tsp. baking soda

Bring margarine, brown sugar, corn syrup and salt to a boil in a small saucepan, stirring constantly. Boil 5 minutes without stirring. Remove from heat and blend in baking soda. Place popped corn and nuts in a large bowl and pour over the sugar/margarine mixture, stirring to coat completely. Spread in a single layer on a cookie sheet. Bake in preheated 200° oven for 1 hour, turning popped corn every 15 minutes. Remove from oven (mixture will still be sticky until it cools completely). Store in a container with tight-fitting lid.

(Note: 1/3 cup unpopped corn makes an ample 2 quarts of popped corn.)

CRUNCH 'N MUNCH POPCORN WITH PEANUTS

1-1/2 qts. popped corn, white or yellow
3/4 cup roasted peanuts, salted or unsalted
1/4 cup (1/2 stick) margarine
1/4 cup honey
1/2 tsp. salt (ONLY if using unsalted peanuts)

Melt honey, margarine, and salt in a small saucepan. Combine popped corn and peanuts in a large bowl. Add honey/margarine mixture and stir to coat completely. Spread in a single layer on a cookie sheet. Bake in a preheated 300° oven 15 to 20 minutes, stirring once, until dry. Cool. Store in container with tight-fitting lid.

(Note: 1/4 cup unpopped corn makes about 1-1/2 qts. popped corn.)

Variation
Use other nuts such as pecans, walnuts, cashews or combine them with peanuts.

PARTY MIX

There are several packaged party mixes available on grocers' shelves, as well as countless recipes printed by cereal producers who want you to use THEIR products. Make your own and put in it what you like! Here's a basic recipe to vary or build upon:

> 7 cups Chex cereal (corn, rice, wheat) or similar
>   bite-size (not sugar-frosted) cereal
> 1 cup salted, mixed nuts
> 1 cup stick pretzels, broken into 2-inch pieces
> 3 TBS. melted margarine
> 4 tsp. Worcestershire sauce
> 2 tsp. lemon juice
> 1/4 tsp. onion powder
> 1/4 tsp. garlic powder

Combine cereal, nuts, pretzels in a 13 x 9 x 2-inch pan; set aside. Stir remaining ingredients together, pour over cereal mix and toss gently with a spoon until cereal is evenly coated. Bake in a preheated 250° oven approximately 45 minutes, stirring every 15 minutes. Spread on paper towels to cool. Store in container with tight-fitting lid.

Variations
Instead of pretzels, use cheese crackers or other tiny snack crackers or Chinese Crisp Noodles (see recipe). Instead of cereal, use unsalted popcorn. Instead of mixed nuts, use smoked or regular almonds, or walnut or pecan pieces.

SALTED NUTS

2 cups walnut or pecan halves, whole almonds,
    filberts, Brazil nuts, or any combination thereof
2 TBS. margarine
Salt

Place the nuts in a shallow pan with margarine and bake in a preheated 350° oven for about 1/2 hour, stirring occasionally. Bake until lightly browned. Remove the pan from the oven and sprinkle with salt (to taste). Drain them on a paper towel, changing the towel after 3 minutes if necessary to remove excess grease. When cool, store in container with tight-fitting lid.

Variations

For smoky flavor nuts, before baking add 1/4 to 1/2 teaspoon liquid hickory smoke to the baking pan OR after toasting, sprinkle with hickory-smoked salt instead of table salt. For garlic or onion flavor, combine 1/4 to 1/2 teaspoon of either powder with 1 teaspoon salt and sprinkle nuts after removing from oven. For spicy flavor, combine 1/4 teaspoon cayenne pepper and 1/4 teaspoon paprika to 1 teaspoon salt and sprinkle nuts after removing from oven.

SUGAR-ROASTED NUTS

These nuts have not only the intriguing sweet-and-salt taste of commercial honey-roasted nuts, but are spicier. When making them, you can use the nuts of your choice and adjust the spices and salt to your liking.

> 1/2 cup granulated sugar
> 1/4 cup cornstarch
> 2-1/2 tsp. All-purpose Baking Spice (see recipe)
>   OR 1-1/2 tsp. ground cinnamon, 1/2 tsp. ground nutmeg, 1/2 tsp. ground allspice
> 1 egg white
> 2 TBS. cold water
> 4 cups nuts (unsalted roasted peanuts, pecan or walnut halves, almonds, filberts, or any combination thereof)
> 1 tsp. salt

Combine sugar, cornstarch, and spices in a large bowl; add the egg white, water and beat slightly. Add the nuts and stir to coat thoroughly. Using a slotted spoon, spread the nuts on a greased cookie sheet, keeping the nuts separated as much as possible. Bake in a preheated 250° oven for about 1/2 hour. Remove from oven and sprinkle on salt; stir to coat and return to oven for 1 more hour of roasting, stirring once or twice.

Remove nuts from the oven (the mixture will still be soft and gummy). Place them in a colander and gently sift the remaining sugar from them. Let the nuts cool completely (they will become crisp and dry) before storing in container with tight-fitting lid.

NORA'S MINCEMEAT

This is an honest, old-fashioned English mincemeat that contains no meat (horrors!) nor does it require cooking. The brandy takes care of that! Stored in a cool place, it will last, literally, for years.

1 lb. (2-1/2 cups) seedless raisins
1 lb. tart apples, pared, finely diced
1 lb. (3 cups) currants
2 oranges, juice and zest
2 lemons, juice and zest
2 tsp. All-purpose Baking Spice (see recipe) OR 1 tsp.
    EACH ground cinnamon and ground nutmeg
1 lb. (4-1/2 cups) beef suet, chopped or coarsely
    ground
1 lb. (2-1/2 cups) seeded muscat raisins
1/2 lb. mixed candied fruit
1 lb. (2-1/4 cups) granulated sugar
1-1/2 cups brandy

Peel lemons and oranges with a vegetable peeler and puree slightly in a blender along with the juice. Combine all ingredients and store in a covered glass or plastic container. If using a metal lid, place a sheet of plastic wrap between container and lid to prevent eventual rusting. Let stand several days before using. Do not refrigerate.

TENNESSEE BARBECUE DRY SEASONING MIX

Although favored in the Midwest for ribs, this mix is equally good on chicken, lamb, and beef.

1 TBS. table salt
1 TBS. onion powder
1 TBS. garlic powder
1 TBS. ground pepper
1 TBS. ground red pepper
  OR red pepper flakes pulverized in a blender
1 TBS. paprika

Combine all ingredients and store in jar with shaker top and tight-fitting lid. Before cooking meat, moisten with water, sprinkle generously all over with Dry Seasoning Mix; rub in well. Proceed to barbecue over charcoal or broil as usual. Before serving, sprinkle meat very lightly with the Dry Seasoning Mix.

MARINADE/BARBECUE SAUCE

This sauce is ideal for short or long marinating of poultry or any meat, as well as making a fine barbecue basting sauce without the ubiquitous tomato base . . . nor does it need cooking.

1/4 cup salad oil, safflower oil preferred
1/4 cup olive oil
1/2 cup dry, red wine
1 tsp. garlic powder
1/2 tsp. salt
Dash of ground pepper

Combine all ingredients and brush on meat or poultry; marinate for short or long period, according to your desire. When barbecuing or broiling, use to baste during cooking. Store extra sauce in bottle with tight-fitting lid. Do not refrigerate.

Variations
Add any or all of the following to the recipe above:
1 TBS. Prepared Hoi Mustard (see recipe)
1-1/2 tsp. Worcestershire sauce
3/4 tsp. Salad Herbs (see recipe)
OR herbs such as thyme, marjoram, oregano

MISCELLANEOUS STANDBYS

BAKING POWDER

2 TBS. cream of tartar powder
1 TBS. baking soda
1 TBS. cornstarch

Sift ingredients together and store in small container with tight-fitting lid. One teaspoon of this equals 1 teaspoon of commercial baking powder.

SELF-RISING FLOUR

For EACH CUP of all-purpose flour, add:
1-1/2 tsp. Baking Powder (see recipe)
1/2 tsp. salt

Sift flour, Baking Powder, and salt together and store in covered container. Use cup-for-cup in all recipes calling for self-rising flour.

SEMISWEET BAKING CHOCOLATE

7 TBS. granulated sugar
6 TBS. unsweetened cocoa
4 TBS. solid vegetable shortening or cooking oil,
   safflower oil preferred

The ingredients listed above equal one 6-ounce package (1 cup) of semisweet chocolate chips OR 6 squares (1 ounce each) of semisweet chocolate. The easiest way to use in a recipe is to combine the cocoa and sugar with the other dry ingredients called for and add the shortening with the other shortening specified. Margarine or butter are not recommended as they contain water.

SWEET BAKING CHOCOLATE

4 TBS. plus 2 tsp. granulated sugar
4 TBS. unsweetened cocoa
2 TBS. plus 2 tsp. solid vegetable shortening or
   cooking oil, safflower oil preferred

The ingredients listed above equal one 4-ounce bar of sweet cooking chocolate. The easiest way to use in a recipe is to combine the sugar and cocoa with the other dry ingredients specified and add the shortening with the other shortening called for. Margarine or butter are not recommended because they contain water.

UNSWEETENED BAKING CHOCOLATE

3 TBS. unsweetened cocoa
1 TBS. solid vegetable shortening or cooking oil, safflower oil preferred

Use instead of 1 square (1 ounce) unsweetened baking chocolate or 1 envelope (1 ounce) premelted unsweetened chocolate. The easiest way to use in a recipe is to add the cocoa to the other dry ingredients specified and add the shortening to the other shortening called for. Margarine or butter are not recommended as they contain water.

Hints and Helps
To make a batch of this mixture and have it on hand for all recipes calling for unsweetened baking chocolate, see Unsweetened Chocolate Crock recipe.

IN THE FRIDGE

EASY LOW-FAT YOGURT

Most homemade yogurt recipes call for carefully heating yogurt and constantly checking temperature with a kitchen thermometer during preparation. IF YOU HAVE A LIGHT BULB IN YOUR OVEN, here is an easy, uncomplicated way to make your own yogurt

    1 8-oz. container, low-fat plain yogurt
       Label must state: "with active yogurt cultures"
    2 cups instant nonfat dry milk solids
    4 cups water

Close oven door and turn on oven light. (If desired, oven can be heated to approximately 100°, then turned off.) Place dry milk solids in a large bowl, add water and beat with whisk until milk powder is completely dissolved. Add yogurt and beat with whisk until well blended. Cover with plastic wrap and place in oven. Let ferment for about 8 hours, or overnight, until mixture is consistency of custard. (If convenient, whisk mixture again after about 5 hours and return to oven.) After 8 hours, remove from oven, turn off oven light, and whisk culture once again. (It will become thin, but will rethicken when refrigerated.) Store your yogurt in closed container and refrigerate.

Hints and Helps

The whisking during and after the fermenting process prevents a thin layer of water from coming to the surface of the yogurt.

Save a cup of your homemade yogurt in the refrigerator as a starter for your next batch.

Use your yogurt in salad dressings, cooking, or as a substitute for sour cream. To flavor, try honey, brown sugar, or molasses; or add your favorite fruit with a little sugar; or add a dollop of jam or jelly; or mix with Cinnamon Sugar (see recipe); or mix with frozen juice concentrate. Let your creativity flow.

CONDIMENTS

SORT-OF TRADITIONAL BARBECUE SAUCE

Count the number of backyard barbecues in the world. Divide that by two. That's probably the number of Barbecue Sauce recipes floating around. Because the one below contains the "basic" tomato, vinegar, mustard, etc., it is as traditional as one can get.

> 1 TBS. salad oil, safflower oil preferred
> 1/4 cup onion, chopped
> 1/4 cup celery, chopped
> 1/4 cup green pepper, chopped
> 1 garlic clove, minced
>   OR 1/4 tsp. garlic powder
> 1 cup condensed tomato soup
>   OR for more tangy sauce, use Tomato Catsup
>   (see recipe)
> 1 cup water
> 2 TBS. Worcestershire sauce
> 2 TBS. brown sugar
> 2 TBS. lemon juice
> 2 TBS. vinegar
> 2 TBS. Prepared Hot Mustard (see recipe)
> 1/2 tsp. Tabasco
> 1 bay leaf

Heat oil in large saucepan; add vegetables and saute until tender. Add remaining ingredients; bring to a boil and simmer, uncovered, for 30 minutes, stirring occasionally. Cool. Store in refrigerator in covered container.

MINT SAUCE

In England roast lamb or broiled lamb chops would be considered "naked" unless served with Mint Sauce. Perhaps, too, it disguised the strong taste of mutton.

      1/2 cup white vinegar
      1/3 cup granulated sugar
      Fresh mint leaves

In small saucepan, heat vinegar and sugar, stirring until sugar dissolves. Using scissors, snip enough mint leaves coarsely to measure 1/2 cupful. Pour hot vinegar/ sugar mixture over mint; cover and let stand several hours. Before serving, strain sauce, discard mint. Snip more fresh mint leaves coarsely to measure 1/4 cupful; add to sauce. Serve at room temperature. Leftover sauce can be refrigerated indefinitely without straining.

PREPARED MUSTARD

OLD BEN'S HOTSY-TOTSY BRANDY MUSTARD

Once you've tried this mustard, you will never be satisfied with ANY commercial mustard again. It is so simple to make and is such a great "bread-and-butter" gift, you'll find yourself making it often. Luckily, the quantities are easy to double, triple, quadruple, etc.

> 1/2 cup dry mustard
> 1 TBS. all-purpose flour
> 2 TBS. cider vinegar
> 1 TBS. brandy
> 1 TBS. granulated sugar

Stir dry mustard and flour together in a small bowl, blending completely. Gradually stir in 3 tablespoons tepid water. Let stand, stirring occasionally, for 1/2 hour. Add remaining ingredients, one at a time, stirring thoroughly. Store in small jar or container with tight-fitting lid and let ripen for at least one week:

"After making it for 18 years, I have just discovered, if you *do not* like your mustard hot,

Keep it in the cupboard.

"But . . . if you wanna blow off-a your socks,

Keep it in the ice-a box!"

Hints and Helps

If you prepare this often, it pays to purchase dry mustard at your bulk-food store. When storing, if using a metal lid, place a piece of plastic wrap between container and lid, as the fumes from the mustard will rust the metal!

GERMAN MUSTARD

This recipe makes a mild, grainy mustard that even kids raised on that "bright-yellow-mayonnaise-nonmustard-mustard" enjoy.

> 1/3 cup whole mustard seed
> 1/3 cup dry mustard
> 1 cup cider vinegar
> 3 TBS. light corn syrup OR honey
> 2 TBS. dark brown sugar
> 1-1/2 tsp. salt
> 1 tsp. onion powder
> 1/2 tsp. garlic powder
> 1/2 tsp. ground cinnamon
> 1/4 tsp. ground allspice
> 1/8 tsp. ground cloves

In small bowl, combine mustard seed and dry mustard; add 2/3 cup *boiling* water; mix well and set aside for 10 minutes. In small saucepan, combine all remaining ingredients and bring to a boil. Reduce heat and simmer, covered, for 5 minutes; remove from heat. Place mustard and vinegar mixtures in a blender and blend on high speed, occasionally scraping down sides with spatula, until mustard seed is crushed. Pour into container with tight-fitting lid. Can be used immediately; refrigerate to retain flavor.

Variation
For hotter mustard, add tepid (instead of boiling) water to mustard/seeds and set aside for 30 minutes, stirring occasionally. Also cool vinegar mixture well before blending.

QUICK CORN RELISH

The lowly ingredients for this easily prepared condiment cost a pittance. So tell me, why is store-bought Corn Relish platinum-priced?

    1 12-oz. can whole kernel corn
    1 small onion, chopped
    1/2 cup celery, thinly sliced
    1 TBS. EACH green pepper and pimiento,
      both chopped
    1/4 cup vinegar
    1/4 cup brown sugar
    1/2 tsp. EACH celery seed, crushed, and salt
      OR Seasoned Salt (see recipe)
    1/8 tsp. EACH ground turmeric and ground pepper
    Dash of cayenne pepper

Drain corn, reserving 1/4 cup of liquid. In sauce-pan, combine reserved liquid with all other ingredients, except corn. Bring mixture to a boil; reduce heat and simmer 5 minutes. Remove from heat and add corn. Store in refrigerator in container with tight-fitting lid. Makes 2-1/2 cups.

CRANBERRY-ORANGE RELISH

1 12-ounce package of raw cranberries (3 cups)
1 large orange, seeded
  OR 2 large or 3 small lemons, seeded
1 cup granulated sugar

Do not peel orange (or lemons). With food processor, using steel cutting blade, process cranberries, orange (or lemons) only until coarsely ground. (If using food grinder, use medium-grind blade.) Combine with sugar and store in refrigerator in covered container.

SALSA

6 large tomatoes
1 medium onion
3/4 cup chopped green chilis
1 tsp. vinegar
1 tsp. salt

Chilis can be roasted or unroasted. (To roast, place chilis in an ungreased frying pan, preferably iron, and cook over a hot fire, turning frequently, until outside is very slightly browned.) For coarse salsa, chop all ingredients by hand and combine; for smoother salsa, chop fine in food processor using sharp steel blade. Store in refrigerator in covered container. Chilis can be frozen and so can Salsa.

Variation:
Green Chili Salsa
Follow the recipe above, except use either green tomatoes or tart, unpared green apples such as Pippins. If using apples, chop them and heat until just cooked through with 1 tablespoon vinegar added, then proceed as above.

RATGIRL'S QUICK SALSA

1 1-lb. can tomatoes, drained and chopped
1 medium onion, chopped
1 4-oz. can, diced green chilis
1 TBS. vinegar
1 tsp. sugar
1/2 tsp. salt
Tabasco sauce (to taste)

Combine all ingredients and let stand at least 30 minutes at room temperature before refrigerating.

SEAFOOD COCKTAIL SAUCE

Serve as a spicy dipping sauce for shrimp, oysters, clams or crab legs. Or combine with cooked seafood, refrigerate for several hours and serve as a Seafood Cocktail.

1 cup (8 oz.) Spanish-style tomato sauce
1/2 cup chili sauce
1 TBS. horseradish
1 TBS. vinegar
1 TBS. finely chopped onion
    OR 1 tsp. minced dried onion
1 TBS. lemon juice, fresh or bottled
1 tsp. mixed pickling spices tied in a bag
1/4 tsp. garlic powder

Combine all ingredients in a saucepan. Bring to a boil and simmer gently 5 minutes. Remove spice bag. Chill. Store in refrigerator.

QUICK TARTAR SAUCE

1 cup Miracle Whip or similar creamy dressing
   OR sour cream, nonfat preferred
1 to 2 TBS. sweet pickle relish
1/2 tsp. Prepared Hot Mustard (see recipe)
1/4 tsp. onion powder

Combine all ingredients and mix well. Keeps indefinitely in refrigerator.

Variations
One teaspoon dried tarragon can be added as well as up to 1/4 cup chopped green olives. One tablespoon fresh parsley can also be added, but not if sauce is to be refrigerated for a lengthy period.

TERIYAKI SAUCE

3/4 cup vegetable oil, safflower oil preferred
1/2 cup soy sauce
2 TBS. vinegar
2 TBS. honey
1-1/2 tsp. ground ginger
2 tsp. onion powder
1 tsp. garlic powder

Combine all ingredients. Place beef, pork or chicken in a large flat pan and marinade for 1 to 3 hours, turning once or twice. Refrigerate Teriyaki Sauce after use; can be used again and again.

TOMATO CATSUP

As with homemade Tomato Sauce, the cost savings in making your own Tomato Catsup is slight. However, when your (or your neighbors') tomato crop runneth over, you will be well rewarded in making this zesty, spicy Catsup. It is thick, rich and far surpasseth the store-bought kind.

4 lbs. washed, unpeeled ripe tomatoes cut into
    small chunks (makes 11 cups chopped tomatoes)
2 medium-to-large onions cut into small chunks
1 garlic clove minced OR 1/2 tsp. garlic powder
1 cup vinegar
1/4 cup brown sugar, packed
1 tsp. celery seed
1 tsp. salt
1 tsp. paprika
1/2 tsp. ground cloves
1/2 tsp. ground allspice
1/2 tsp. ground mace
1/4 tsp. ground cinnamon
1/4 tsp. ground pepper
2 bay leaves

Place tomatoes and onions in a large, heavy kettle. Bring to a boil and cook uncovered until tender, about 20 minutes. Remove from heat and puree the mixture in a blender, about 2 cups at a time. Return mixture to kettle and add balance of ingredients.

Simmer, uncovered, stirring occasionally, approximately 1-1/2 hours, until mixture is reduced in volume by about 1/3 to 1/2. Cool completely and store in refrigerator in containers with lids. Can be frozen.

REFRIED BEANS

These Refried Beans have three advantages:
(1) A sauciness which you can adjust to your liking. (2) They can be made either from "scratch" or with canned beans. (3) They contain no lard, which today is spelled "cholesterol".

> 1 lb. (2-1/2 cups) dried pinto beans
>   OR 2 1-lb. cans pinto beans
> 1 medium onion, chopped
> 1 tsp. Serious Chili Powder (see recipe)
>   OR 1 TBS. chili powder
> 1 TBS. olive oil
> 1 tsp. salt OR Seasoned Salt (see recipe)
> 1 tsp. ground cumin
> 1 tsp. Serious Chili Powder
>   OR 1 TBS. chili powder
> 1 tsp. Seasoned Salt OR 1 tsp. salt
> 1/2 tsp. cayenne pepper
>   (omit if using Serious Chili Powder)
> Salsa to taste (see recipe)

If using dried pintos:

Wash beans and combine with onion, 1 tablespoon chili powder (or 1 teaspoon Serious Chili Powder), olive oil, and 1 teaspoon salt. Add water to cover and soak overnight. Do not drain; add more water if necessary just to cover and cook beans until tender. Add cumin, second teaspoon salt, second tablespoon chili powder (or 1 teaspoon Serious Chili Powder), cayenne, and Salsa and mash with potato masher or fork, leaving some beans intact. All liquid should be absorbed; add water if necessary to attain the desired consistency.

If using canned pintos:

Saute onion in olive oil with 1 teaspoon salt and 1 tablespoon chili powder (or 1 teaspoon Serious Chili

Powder). Add undrained beans, cumin, second table-spoon chili powder (or 1 teaspoon Serious Chili Powder), cayenne, and Salsa. Do not add the second teaspoon of salt. Follow above procedure for mashing.

BEAN DIP

2 cups Refried Beans (see recipe)
   OR 1 15-ounce can refried beans
2 TBS. onion, or scallions, minced
1 TBS. cooking oil, safflower oil preferred
1 7-ounce can diced green chilis
1/2 cup (2 oz.) shredded Monterey Jack cheese
Sour cream, sliced ripe olives (optional)

Saute onion in oil until tender. Add beans, diced chilis, shredded cheese and cook, stirring, until cheese begins to melt and mixture is hot. Garnish with sour cream and sliced ripe olives if desired. Serve with Tortilla Chips (see recipe). (Can also be served at room temperature.)

SHIRLEY'S GARLIC SPREAD

This is to store-bought garlic spread as Tiffany's is to Woolworth's. Moreover, it's worth going out and buying chervil, just so you can use it in this "mouth-melter".

> 4 sticks (1 lb.) margarine
> 2 large garlic cloves
> 1/4 tsp. Seasoned Salt (see recipe)
>   OR 1/4 tsp. salt
> 2 tsp. chervil
> 2 tsp. savory
> 1 tsp. tarragon
> 1 tsp. basil

Cream margarine. Push garlic through press (or mash with back of spatula) and combine with salt. Crush herbs slightly in mortar with pestle. Blend margarine, garlic, and herbs thoroughly and let stand at room temperature for at least 2 hours. Store in container with tight-fitting lid. Can be frozen.

To prepare:

(1) Spread on a half loaf of French bread cut lengthwise. If desired, sprinkle on Romano cheese, sesame and poppy seeds, and paprika. Toast under broiler until brown; watch carefully as it can burn easily.

(2) Cut a loaf of French bread into very thin slices. Do not slice all the way through; leave the bottom crust undisturbed. Spread a little of Shirley's Garlic Spread on each slice. Place loaf in a paper bag, closing the top. Bake in a preheated 350° oven about 20 minutes or until lightly browned and heated through.

TRADITIONAL GARLIC SPREAD

2 sticks (1/2 lb.) margarine
4 large garlic cloves
1/2 tsp. Seasoned Salt (see recipe) OR salt

Cream margarine. Push garlic through press (or mash with back of spatula) and combine with salt. Thoroughly blend margarine and garlic/salt. Refrigerate. Can be frozen.

To prepare:
See Shirley's Garlic Spread above.

DILLED GREEN BEANS

Store-bought dilled beans seem to be priced by the carat! Make your own and enjoy them as a relish, in salads, or better yet, as a replacement for the olive in a martini!

1 lb. green beans
1/4 cup wine vinegar
1 TBS. salt
2 tsp. dried red sweet pepper
1/2 tsp. dill weed,
   slightly crushed in mortar with pestle
1/4 tsp. garlic powder

Wash and trim ends from beans; leave them long enough to pack lengthwise into a tall glass jar (peanut butter jars work quite well). Cook beans in boiling water until just tender. Combine balance of ingredients and bring to a boil in small saucepan. Drain beans and pack vertically into jars as indicated above. Fill with dilled vinegar mixture and cover with tight-fitting lid. Refrigerate for at least 24 hours before using.

Hints and Helps
A one-pound can of vertical-pack blue lake green beans, well drained, can be substituted for fresh beans, but you will find them rather "dear".

PICKLED MUSHROOMS (CANNED)

2 6-ounce cans mushroom caps
1 cup vinegar
3/4 cup dark brown sugar, packed
2 tsp. whole pickling spices

Drain mushrooms, reserving 1/2 cup liquid. Combine reserved liquid with balance of ingredients in small saucepan and simmer, uncovered, for 5 minutes. Pour over mushrooms; cover and refrigerate for 2 days. To serve, drain mushrooms, place a toothpick in each.

Hints and Helps
Leftover mushrooms will keep longer in the refrigerator if again covered with the pickling liquid drained from them before they were first served.

PICKLED MUSHROOMS (FRESH)

1 lb. small mushroom caps, cleaned
1/4 cup olive oil
3 TBS. white vinegar
2 tsp. whole pickling spices
1/2 tsp. salt
1/2 bay leaf
1/4 tsp. garlic powder

Combine all ingredients, except mushrooms, in an enameled, heat-proof glass, or stainless steel saucepan; bring to a boil. Add mushrooms, cover, and simmer very gently for 5 minutes. Cool completely and place in a glass or plastic container with lid. Add just enough water to cover mushrooms; cover container and keep at room temperature for 2 days. Store mushrooms and liquid in container in refrigerator until served. To serve, drain mushrooms, place a toothpick in each.

Variations
Add 1/4 teaspoon dried thyme and 1/4 teaspoon dried oregano. Also, 10 black peppercorns can be substituted for the pickling spices.

Hints and Helps
Leftover mushrooms will keep longer in the refrigerator if stored in their pickling liquid.

PICKLED BEETS

10 small, unpeeled beets
  OR 1 1-lb. can whole or sliced beets
1/2 cup vinegar
1/2 cup water
2 TBS. granulated sugar
1 TBS. minced dried onion
2 tsp. whole peppercorns
1 tsp. whole mustard seeds
1 bay leaf
1/2 tsp. salt

If using fresh beets, boil in unsalted water until tender (20 to 40 minutes). Cool in cooking water, then slip off the skins; cut in slices or quarters. If using canned beets, drain, then cut in slices or quarters. Bring vinegar, water, and rest of ingredients to a boil and simmer 5 minutes; cool slightly. Place beets in a jar and add the vinegar/spice mixture. If necessary, add more vinegar mixed with equal amount of water just to cover. Let sit, covered, at room temperature for 24 hours. Store in the refrigerator.

SPICED PEACHES

1 large (1-lb. 13-oz.) can peach halves or slices
2 TBS. cinnamon "Red Hots" candies,
    OR 4 or 5 cinnamon "Fire" candies, crushed
1 TBS. lemon juice, fresh or bottled

Drain peaches and pour liquid into a small sauce-pan. Add candy and lemon juice, and cook stirring, just until candy is completely melted. Let cool slightly and pour over the peaches. Chill, covered, overnight or longer. Store in refrigerator in container with tight-fitting lid.

Hints and Helps

To crush "Fire" candies, place in the corner of a plastic grocery bag, fold bag over candy several times, and smack smartly with a hammer.

SAUSAGES

HERB SAUSAGE

1 lb. ground beef
3 TBS. grated Parmesan cheese
2 TBS. dry red wine
1-1/2 level tsp. Morton Tender Quick curing salt
1 tsp. EACH ground pepper, crushed dried basil,
    crushed dried oregano
1/2 tsp. mustard seeds
1/4 tsp. EACH onion powder, garlic powder

Combine all ingredients, mixing until thoroughly blended. Divide in half. Shape each half into a firm, slender roll approximately 1-1/2 inches in diameter. Wrap in plastic and refrigerate overnight. Unwrap and place on rack in broiler pan and bake at 200° for 4 hours. When cool, store wrapped in refrigerator. Use within 3 to 5 days or freeze for later use. If frozen bring to room temperature before slicing.

Hints and Helps

Buy the cheapest ground beef you can find; it works best! Morton Tender Quick curing salt is available in the canning section of some groceries or in specialty shops carrying home meat-curing products. If you can't find it, send a blank check (I don't have the latest price) for a 2-pound package to Cumberland General Store, Route 3, Crossville, TN 38555. Allow 4 to 6 weeks for delivery. It is well worth the effort!

BEEF SALAMI

1 lb. ground beef
1-1/2 level tsp. Morton Tender Quick curing salt
1 tsp. salt
1/2 tsp. EACH mustard seeds, ground pepper, and
  garlic powder
1/4 tsp. liquid smoke
1/8 tsp. ground nutmeg

Prepare exactly the same as for Herb Sausage. See also: Hints and Helps.

PEPPERONI

1 lb. ground beef
1-1/2 level tsp. Morton Tender Quick curing salt
1 tsp. liquid smoke
3/4 tsp. ground pepper
1/2 tsp. EACH mustard seeds, fennel seeds and
  red pepper flakes, crushed
1/4 tsp. EACH anise seeds and garlic powder

Prepare exactly the same as for Herb Sausage. See also: Hints and Helps.

SLOPPY JOES

These saucy skilletburgers are so good and easy to prepare, you'll wonder why you ever opened a can of store-bought stuff.

> 1-1/2 lbs. lean ground beef
> 1 TBS. olive or salad oil, safflower oil preferred
> 1 cup Salsa (see recipe)
> 1/4 cup Tomato Catsup (see recipe)
> 1/2 tsp. Seasoned Salt (see recipe)
> 1 tsp. Prepared Hot Mustard (see recipe)

Saute beef in hot oil in large frying pan. Add balance of ingredients and simmer, uncovered, 5 to 10 minutes.

TRADITIONAL SLOPPY JOES

This more conventional Sloppy Joe recipe features items that are surely in every kitchen, right?

> 1-1/2 lbs. ground beef
> 1 medium onion, chopped
> 1 tsp. Seasoned Salt (see recipe) OR salt
> 1/2 cup Tomato Catsup (see recipe)
> 2 TBS. Prepared Hot Mustard (see recipe)
> 2 TBS. brown sugar
> 2 TBS. Worcestershire sauce
> 1/4 tsp. liquid smoke (optional)

Brown beef and onion with salt in frying pan; drain off excess fat, if necessary. Add remaining ingredients and simmer 5 to 10 minutes.

PATÉ 1 (CHICKEN LIVERS)

When you serve either of these Patés and someone asks, "Is it French?" you can reply, "No, it's like my guests: domestic or, at least, domesticated."

    1/2 lb. chicken livers
    2 TBS. margarine
    2 pkgs. (3-oz. each) cream cheese,
      regular or reduced calorie
    3 eggs, hard-boiled
    1 TBS. brandy
    3/4 tsp. Seasoned Salt (see recipe)
      OR salt
Dash ground pepper

    Saute chicken livers in margarine until they are pink, about 5 minutes (overcooked livers become dry). In food processor, using steel blade, combine livers/ margarine with balance of ingredients and process until smooth. Refrigerate, covered, until needed.

PATÉ 2 (LIVERWURST)

    1 lb. liverwurst OR Braunschweiger,
      cut in 1-in. pieces
    1/4 small onion, chopped
    1/2 cup sour cream, nonfat preferred
    1/4 cup brandy
    1 tsp. Prepared Hot Mustard (see recipe)

    In food processor, using steel blade, process all ingredients until smooth. Refrigerate, covered, until needed.

CHEDDAR CHEESE BALLS

2 cups (8 oz.) Cheddar cheese, shredded
1 package (8-oz.) cream cheese, reduced calorie
   preferred
 4 TBS. margarine, softened
1 tsp. Worcestershire sauce
1/2 tsp. onion powder
1/4 tsp. garlic powder
1/4 tsp. paprika
1/2 cup nuts, chopped

Combine all ingredients, except nuts, in bowl and mix thoroughly with a fork. Cover and refrigerate until well chilled. Form into 1 or 2 large cheese balls and roll in chopped nuts.

Hints and Helps

Balls that have been partially consumed can be reformed into balls and rolled again in chopped nuts; your next round of guests will never know the difference. Can be frozen; if so, bring to room temperature before serving.

TOMATO SAUCE

As canned tomato sauce is so inexpensive and contains no chemical additives, the only justification for making your own is when tomatoes are in full season and market prices are rock-bottom, or if you are blessed with a bountiful harvest.

    3 TBS. olive oil
    1 large or 2 medium onions, chopped
    1/2 small green pepper, chopped
    2 celery stalks with leaves, chopped
    1 carrot, finely chopped
    2 garlic cloves, chopped
    4 cups ripe, unpeeled tomatoes, chopped
    1 tsp. brown sugar
    1 tsp. Seasoned Salt (see recipe) OR salt
    1 tsp. dried basil
    1/4 tsp. ground pepper

Heat olive oil in a large, heavy saucepan. Add onion, green pepper, celery, carrot, and garlic and cook, stirring, for about 5 minutes. Add tomatoes and balance of ingredients and simmer the sauce gently until thick, about 45 minutes to 1 hour. Put mixture through a fine strainer or puree in the blender; adjust seasonings if necessary. Refrigerate in glass container (plastic reacts to the tomatoes); can be frozen.

SWEETENED CONDENSED MILK

How frustrating to come across an enticing recipe that demands this kind of canned milk and you don't keep any on the pantry shelf. Not only can you make it yourself, but you'll save more than half the cost!

    2 cups instant nonfat dry milk solids
    1-1/2 cups granulated sugar
    3/4 cup boiling water
    6 TBS. melted margarine

Combine the dry milk and sugar, then gradually add the boiling water. Stir in the melted margarine. Whip with a whisk or in a blender until smooth. Refrigerate in container with tight-fitting lid. Can be frozen.

"CREAM" CHEESE

The Good News: This "Cream" Cheese has about one-half the calories, one-third the fat, and twice the protein of commercial cream cheese and costs less than half as much. It also has a more interesting texture, as compared to the "slick" store-bought kind.

The Bad News: It is virtually the only prepared food in this book which has a long preparation time. You won't be occupied all that time, but it does take 2 to 4 hours to drain. Also, it is one of the few recipes calling for a kitchen thermometer.

    1 gal. (4 qts.) whole milk
    1 qt. cultured buttermilk
    1 tsp. salt

In a large pan, combine milk and buttermilk; add a kitchen thermometer to side of pan. Heat, stirring occasionally, until the temperature registers 170°. Keeping the temperature at between 170° and 175° maximum, continue heating until thick curds begin separating from the whey, about 1/2 hour.

While the mixture is heating, line a colander with 3 or 4 layers of moistened cheesecloth; set colander in a large bowl and place beside the cooking pan. As large curds form, lift them with a slotted spoon onto the cheesecloth. When all the largest curds have been removed, gently pour the remaining curds and whey into the colander. Discard the whey.* Permit curds to drain, at room temperature for 2 to 4 hours. Scrape the cheese from the cloth and mix in salt with a fork. Cheese will have the consistency of ricotta, but if you like it smooth, process in blender or electric mixer at slow speed.

Cover and refrigerate. Makes about 4 cups or 2 pounds of cheese. Cheese can also be frozen; thaw completely and beat with mixer at low speed.

*Rather than pouring the whey down the sink, I chilled it and found it absolutely delicious to drink. But then, I . . .

SOURDOUGH STARTER

Those Con Artists who sell packets of dry sourdough starter as though it were a magic potion rank with those who offer Beer Bread (see recipe) "kits".

2/3 cup of all-purpose flour
2/3 cup warm water
1 tsp. active dry yeast

Prepare Sourdough Starter 24 hours ahead. Mix flour, water, and yeast in a large pottery, glass, or plastic bowl, making sure bowl is filled only halfway. Cover bowl with plastic wrap and put it in a warm place (about 80° - inside the oven with the oven light turned on is an ideal place). The next day the mixture is ready to use in any sourdough recipe. Leftover Sourdough Starter can be kept in a tightly covered glass or plastic container in the refrigerator. When liquid rises to the top, mix gently with a fork to blend before using.

WHIPPED "CREAM"

If you don't have whipped cream on hand (and, who does?) this makes a fast, low-calorie and easy substitute IF you use chilled equipment and cold liquid, and IF your Whipped "Cream" is used within about 1/2 hour of preparation.

> 1/2 cup instant nonfat dry milk solids
> 1/2 cup ice-cold water OR milk
> 2 TBS. lemon juice (for a more stable foam)
> 1/4 cup granulated sugar

Put dry milk solids in a small, cold bowl and add ice-cold liquid. Using cold beaters, beat with electric mixer at high speed about 4 to 5 minutes until soft peaks form. Add lemon juice and continue beating. Add sugar gradually and beat an additional 2 to 3 minutes until stiff. Chill. Use within 1/2 hour. Makes about 2-1/2 cups.

UNSWEETENED CHOCOLATE CROCK

Chocolate in any form, like coffee, has become an expensive item. By making your own Chocolate Crock to use instead of unsweetened chocolate squares or envelopes of premelted chocolate, you will save up to 40 percent. Moreover, when baking, it need not be melted before incorporating with the other ingredients.

    1 can (8 oz.) unsweetened cocoa
    1 cup solid vegetable shortening

Combine ingredients in a bowl and mash into a paste. Place paste in a container with tight-fitting lid and refrigerate until ready to use. Use 2 tablespoons of your Chocolate Crock mixture for each square (1 ounce) of unsweetened chocolate. Makes 2 cups, equivalent to two 8-ounce packages of unsweetened chocolate.

INSTANT FROZEN VEGETABLES

Freeze vegetables only if they are to be used in cooking. They should be used without thawing by braising or using in soups and stews.

Onions, celery, peppers, mushrooms, scallions

Chop cleaned vegetables to desired fineness, then place in a single layer on baking sheet or large pie pan. Cover with plastic wrap and freeze until firm. Spoon immediately into plastic freezer containers or plastic freezer bags, seal tightly, label, and return to freezer. When needed in cooking, spoon out desired quantity and return balance to freezer.

Peas, lima beans, corn, asparagus, carrots, broccoli, green beans

Peas, limas and corn kernels can be frozen whole; the other listed vegetables should be cleaned, then cut into bite-size pieces, then frozen and stored as indicated above.

Note:
Tomatoes, cucumbers, zucchini, spinach, lettuce, kale, and cabbage should not be frozen at home.

HERBS AND SPICES

SEASONED SALT

1 cup salt
2-1/2 tsp. celery seed crushed slightly in mortar
   with pestle
2 tsp. onion powder
1 tsp. garlic powder
1 tsp. paprika
1/2 tsp. oregano
1/2 tsp. pepper
1/4 tsp. thyme
1/4 tsp. anise seed crushed slightly in mortar
   with pestle

Combine all ingredients and store on spice shelf in container with tight-fitting lid.

Hints and Helps
Use Kosher salt, if desired, rather than regular table salt. It has a coarser texture, and I think it has a better flavor.

OLD GER'S SALT-FREE SEASONING MIX

Combine equal portions of:

Onion powder
Garlic powder
Celery seed, slightly crushed in mortar with pestle
Paprika
Chili powder
Ground pepper
Ground nutmeg

Blend ingredients thoroughly and store in small jar with shaker top and tight-fitting lid. Use as a substitute whenever salt is specified.

SALAD HERBS

4 tsp. EACH of dried . . .
Basil
Chervil (optional)
Marjoram
Oregano
Rosemary
Sage
Savory
Thyme

Combine all ingredients and store on spice shelf in container with tight-fitting lid. Just before using, if desired, crush with mortar and pestle to release flavors.

Hints and Helps

Buy your herbs and spices from a bulk food store in quantities of 1 or 2 ounces. You'll save money and freshness is no problem because of rapid store turnover.

POULTRY SEASONING

1 cup powdered sage
1/2 cup dried marjoram crushed in mortar
    with pestle
1/3 cup powdered rosemary
    OR 1/2 cup dried rosemary powdered in blender
2 tsp. onion powder
1/2 tsp. ground ginger

Combine all ingredients and store on spice shelf in container with tight-fitting lid.

ALL-PURPOSE BAKING SPICE
(Pumpkin Pie Spice)

This flavorful combination deserves to be called more than just Pumpkin Pie Spice because it adds real zest to fruit pies and crisps, in cakes, cookies, bran muffins, waffles and pancakes, sprinkled on cooked sweet potatoes or yams, and on all yellow squashes and carrots. Also, add a pinch to each cup of freshly brewed coffee.

3 TBS. ground cinnamon
1-1/2 tsp. ground ginger
1 tsp. ground nutmeg
1 tsp. ground allspice
1/2 to 1 tsp. ground mace
1/4 tsp. ground cloves

Combine all ingredients and store in a small jar with tight-fitting lid.

CURRY POWDER

The money saved by mixing your own Curry Powder is minimal. The reward is that making it is fun and so immensely SATISFYING.

The dictionary defines curry powder as "a powdered condiment of pungent spices, turmeric, etc." That "etc." is your license to wing it.

Here are just some of the accepted ingredients for curry powder: allspice, anise, bay leaves, caraway, cardamom, celery seed, chili, cinnamon, cloves, coriander, cumin, dill, fennel, fenugreek, garlic, ginger, mace, mustard, nutmeg, onion, oregano, paprika, pepper (white, black and red), poppy seed, saffron, and turmeric.

You can't go wrong by adding a smidgen of your favorites to a basic curry powder recipe. Here is one that should please all palates:

SAHIB BEN'S CURRY POWDER

1 TBS. plus 1 tsp. ground cumin
1 TBS. ground turmeric
1 TBS. ground coriander
1 TBS. ground ginger
1 TBS. ground fenugreek
   OR 1 TBS. fenugreek seeds
1-1/2 tsp. ground cinnamon
1-1/2 tsp. dry mustard
1 tsp. ground cardamom
1 tsp. dill weed
1/2 tsp. cayenne pepper
1/8 tsp. ground allspice
1/8 tsp. ground cloves

If ground fenugreek is not available, combine seeds in blender along with dill weed and reduce to a powder; otherwise, crush dill weed in mortar with pestle. Combine all ingredients and store on spice shelf in container with tight-fitting lid.

SERIOUS CHILI POWDER

Making this Chili Powder is well worth the effort! It brings chili con carne and other Mexican dishes a pungent, fresher taste than with packaged chili powders. Nor does it mask the flavors of the other ingredients with a too heavy chili taste. However, proceed with caution! When blending, using rubber gloves is suggested; also do not breathe in the "dust" and "fumes" from the mixture in the blender, as runny nose and eyes can result.

    3 TBS. freshly ground, dried chilis (see below)
    1 TBS. ground cumin
    1 tsp. paprika
    1 tsp. dried oregano, crushed
    1/4 tsp. garlic powder
    1/4 tsp. ground coriander
    1/8 tsp. ground allspice
    1/8 tsp. ground turmeric
    1/8 tsp. ground cloves

A 1-ounce package of tiny, dried chili pods will make a scant 5-1/2 tablespoons of chili powder. Drop pods in blender, cover, and blend at high speed until pulverized. Leave blender covered a few minutes until "dust" settles in bottom; also tap sides of blender to help powder on sides drop to the bottom. Carefully (see Caution above) measure 3 tablespoons freshly ground chili powder into a small bowl. Combine with balance of ingredients and store in small jar with tight-fitting lid. Makes 4-1/2 tablespoons.

Use sparingly in chili con carne and enchiladas, tacos, flautas, dips, etc. If you are accustomed to adding 3 tablespoons commercial chili powder to chili con carne, use 2 *teaspoons or less* Serious Chili Powder to start. You can always add more.

INTERNATIONAL SPICE MIXES

Check those rows and rows of spice packets. How can it be legal to charge close to a dollar for a tiny envelope of "foreign" spice blends when the first ingredient is either salt or enriched wheat flour? Make your own for a pittance, and know what goes into them.

ITALIAN SEASONING MIX

4 TBS. dried oregano
2 tsp. dried basil
2 tsp. minced dried onion
1 tsp. minced dried garlic

Combine all ingredients lightly and store in spice jar with lid. Use in spaghetti sauces, minestrone, casseroles, or sprinkle on salads.

MEXICAN SEASONING MIX

2 TBS. dried oregano
1 TBS. dried marjoram
1 TBS. ground cumin
1 tsp. Serious Chili Powder (see recipe)
 OR 2 tsp. chili powder
2 tsp. minced dried onion
1 tsp. All-purpose Baking Spice (see recipe)
 OR 1 tsp. ground cinnamon

Combine all ingredients lightly and store in spice jar with lid. Use in enchilada sauce, in tacos, flautas, taco salad, guacamole dip and chili salsa con queso.

GREEK SEASONING MIX

2 TBS. All-purpose Baking Spice (see recipe)
OR 1 TBS. ground cinnamon, 1 tsp. ground
nutmeg,
1 tsp. ground allspice
2 TBS. dried thyme
2 tsp. dried lemon peel
2 tsp. minced dried garlic

Combine all ingredients lightly and store in spice jar with lid. Use in moussaka, meat sauce, and on roasted or stewed chicken.

FRENCH SEASONING MIX

2 TBS. dried thyme
2 TBS. dried tarragon
2 bay leaves, broken up
2 tsp. dried oregano
2 tsp. dried basil

Combine all ingredients lightly and store in spice jar with lid. Use in casseroles, soups, sauces, and on roasted meats and fowl.

CINNAMON SUGAR

My youngest brother, Gerry, would not have survived childhood had he been deprived of his daily buttered breakfast toast dusted with Cinnamon Sugar. I am surprised he does not have red hair.

> 6 TBS. granulated sugar
> 2 tsp. ground cinnamon

Combine and store in container with tight-fitting lid, preferably with a shaker top. Sprinkle on buttered toast, French toast, pancakes and waffles, on cooked cereal, puddings, plain yogurt and ice cream.

Variations

When preparing, add 1/4 teaspoon ground nutmeg OR ground allspice to the basic recipe.

DRIED ORANGE PEEL

Some of the spiced coffee recipes herein call for dried orange peel, and it is essential for really good rye bread. Your mixture will come out aromatic and colorful, as compared to the insipid and expensive store-bought kind.

5 or more large oranges (it doesn't pay to do even this simple task for less)

Wash and dry oranges. Peel them, using a vegetable peeler (then use the rest of the orange for juice or sticky-finger eating). Spread peel on a cookie sheet and dry on top shelf of oven heated to 200° for about 1-1/2 hours; toss peel once or twice during the drying. Remove from oven and place about a handful of peel at a time in a blender. Blend until fine, then return peel to cookie sheet and continue to dry for another 1/2 hour. Cool to room temperature. Place in small jar with tight-fitting lid. Just before using, crush peel in mortar with pestle to give an added burst of flavor and aroma.

VANILLA EXTRACT

Vanilla beans currently cost a minimum of $2.50 each! Despite this, you will save substantially by making your own extract; moreover, when the mixture gets low, you can add more vodka, almost ad infinitum.

    1 vanilla bean, cut into 1-inch pieces
    1 cup vodka
    1/2 tsp. granulated sugar

Combine 2/3 cup of the vodka, vanilla bean, and sugar in a blender and blend until bean is pulverized as much as possible. Line a small strainer with a piece of coffee filter paper or a small piece of muslin. Place strainer in a small bowl and pour liquid through. Slosh out blender bowl with remaining 1/3 cup of the vodka and again pour through strainer. Carefully draw edges of filter paper or cloth together and tie with thread to form a packet containing the pulverized bean. Pour vodka into a small jar, add the bean packet, and close with a tight-fitting lid. Store for one week, shaking occasionally, before using.

Variation
For a smooth, slightly different flavor, use light rum instead of vodka.

SALAD DRESSINGS AND SALADS

SALAD DRESSINGS

Most of the following salad dressings are low in calories. Although hundreds of salad dressings abound, very few have reduced calories. Some use gelatin to replace high-calorie salad oil, and they just aren't good!

One "secret" ingredient is liquid pectin, available in the food-canning section of groceries. It not only replaces oil as a "thickening" agent, but has the added advantage of fighting cholesterol!

Another is the use of Miracle Whip or similar creamy salad dressing instead of mayonnaise: It has 1/3 less fat and 1/3 less calories.

BEN'S BASIC FRENCH DRESSING

1/3 cup vinegar. Fill the cup to half-way mark with
   red/white wine OR water
1-1/2 tsp. granulated sugar
1 tsp. Seasoned Salt (see recipe) OR salt
1 tsp. onion powder
1/2 tsp. EACH garlic powder, dry mustard, Salad
   Herbs (see recipe)
1/4 tsp. ground pepper
2 TBS. olive or salad oil, safflower oil preferred
1 TBS. liquid pectin

In small jar, with lid, combine vinegar and wine (or
water) and all dry ingredients. Pour oil and liquid pectin
in measuring cup, then fill to half-way mark with water;
combine with the vinegar mixture. Cover and shake thoroughly to blend. Do NOT refrigerate; keeps indefinitely.

Hints and Helps
Liquid pectin comes in two foil packets. Open top
and squeeze into small bottle and store in the refrigerator for using in making low-calories dressings. Keeps
indefinitely.

LOW-CALORIE MUSTARD
VINAIGRETTE DRESSING

Ben's Basic French Dressing (see recipe), omitting
   the herbs
2 TBS. Prepared Hot or German Mustard
   (see recipes)

Combine ingredients in small jar with lid. Shake
thoroughly to blend. Do NOT refrigerate.

LOW-CALORIE HONEY-MUSTARD DRESSING

1/3 cup vinegar. Fill the cup to half-way mark
  with water
3 TBS. honey
2 TBS. Prepared Hot Mustard (see recipe)
2 TBS. olive or salad oil, safflower oil preferred
2 TBS. liquid pectin
2 TBS. water
1 tsp. onion powder
1/2 tsp. garlic powder
1/2 tsp. celery seed, crushed slightly in mortar
  with pestle
1/4 tsp. salt
1/4 tsp. ground pepper

Combine all ingredients in small jar with lid. Shake
thoroughly to blend. Do NOT refrigerate.

BUTTERMILK SALAD DRESSING

1/4 cup buttermilk powder
1-1/2 tsp. granulated sugar
1 tsp. EACH salt, onion powder
1/2 tsp. EACH garlic powder, dry mustard, Salad
  Herbs (see recipe)
1/4 tsp. ground pepper
1/2 cup water
1 cup Miracle Whip or similar creamy salad dressing

Combine dry ingredients thoroughly in a small bowl.
Add water and whip thoroughly with whisk or fork until
well blended. Add salad dressing and whip again. Store
in refrigerator in covered container.

CREAMY ROQUEFORT DRESSING

1 8-oz. package reduced calorie cream cheese
1 3-oz. package Roquefort OR Blue Cheese
3/4 cup nonfat milk
1/4 cup Miracle Whip
   OR similar creamy salad dressing

Mix well with a fork and store in refrigerator in covered container.

MILLIE'S "MAYONNAISE"

Virtually all the recipes in this book are fast and fun to make and easy as well. Making regular mayonnaise is both tricky and time-consuming. Here is a no-fail recipe which has a more interesting texture than regular mayonnaise. Use it like mayonnaise and in all recipes where creamy salad dressing is called for.

2 TBS. all-purpose flour
2 TBS. granulated sugar
1 tsp. salt
1 tsp. dry mustard
Dash cayenne pepper
3/4 cup nonfat milk
2 egg yolks, slightly beaten
1 TBS. margarine
1/4 cup white vinegar
1/4 cup olive or salad oil, safflower oil preferred

Combine dry ingredients. Add milk and egg yolks and cook in double boiler until thick, stirring constantly. Turn off heat; add margarine, vinegar and oil and beat until smooth. When cool, refrigerate in container with tight-fitting lid.

TOMATO "FRENCH" DRESSING

That bottle of pink salad gunk on the grocer's shelf is no more French than are those long, slim, deep-fried potatoes that bear their name. The merest mention of this bland concoction reduces salad epicures to tears.

However . . . when I grew up in the Midwest, even the most elegant restaurants served an upright wedge of "iceberg" lettuce garnished with a generous splash of this pink stuff. As a result, one can become hooked, and secretly pine for a large slab of ice-cold, knife-cut, nondescript head lettuce awash in thin, pink cream.

Fortunately, here is a so-called Tomato "French" Dressing with an interesting texture and real get-up-and-go which you will be proud to serve to your guests, perhaps barring an epicure or two:

    1 10-1/2 oz. can condensed tomato soup
    1 cup vinegar (any kind)
    1/2 cup olive or salad oil, safflower oil preferred
    1/4 cup granulated sugar
    1 TBS. Worcestershire sauce
    2 tsp. Seasoned Salt (see recipe) OR salt
    1 tsp. dry mustard
    1 tsp. onion powder
    1/2 tsp. garlic powder
    1/2 tsp. paprika
    1/2 tsp. ground pepper

Combine all ingredients in jar with lid; shake well to blend. Chill and shake well before serving. Store in refrigerator.

YOGURT-DILL DRESSING

This low-calorie dressing combines low-fat yogurt with Miracle Whip (or similar) creamy dressing which has 1/3 less fat and 1/3 less calories than mayonnaise.

1 cup Low-fat Yogurt (see recipe)
1 cup Miracle Whip or similar creamy dressing
1 TBS. dill weed
1-1/2 tsp. granulated sugar
1 tsp. Seasoned Salt (see recipe) OR salt
1 tsp. onion powder
1/2 tsp. garlic powder
1/2 tsp. dry mustard
1/4 tsp. ground pepper

Blend all ingredients in a small bowl with whisk or fork. Store in refrigerator in covered container.

MIXED BEAN SALAD

The particular advantage (aside from the do-it-yourself-savings) of making your own Mixed Bean Salad is that you can use only your favorite beans. This recipe gives you a wide choice!

2 cans (1 lb. each) red kidney beans, drained
1 can (1 lb.) square-cut green beans, drained
1 can (1 lb.) yellow wax beans, drained
1 can (1 lb.) green lima beans, drained
1 cup garbanzo beans, drained
2 TBS. minced dried onion
2 tsp. Seasoned Salt (see recipe)
Ben's Basic French Dressing
   OR Tomato "French" Dressing (see recipe)

If necessary, cut the beans into bite-size pieces. Combine all the beans, onion, and Seasoned Salt in a large bowl and dress — *but don't drown* — with either style of French Dressing. Spoon into wide-mouth jars; cover with tight-fitting lid and refrigerate several hours before serving.

Hints and Helps
If well-dressed, this salad will keep for weeks in the refrigerator. Therefore, it is advisable to cover the jars with a sheet of plastic wrap before closing (as metal lids will begin to rust). Before serving, invert the jar(s) in the refrigerator for about 1/2 hour to let the dressing recoat the beans.

TOMATO ASPIC

Canned aspics have a spiritless, somewhat metallic flavor and uninteresting texture that is an affront to even the most plebeian palate. Here are two easy aspics to remedy that situation:

        2-1/4 cups vegetable juice cocktail
            OR tomato juice
        1 envelope unflavored gelatin
        1 TBS. vinegar
        1-1/2 tsp. prepared horseradish
        1 tsp. granulated sugar
        1 tsp. minced dried onion
        3/4 tsp. Seasoned Salt (see recipe) OR salt
        1/2 tsp. Worcestershire sauce

   Soften gelatin in the 1/4 cup of juice in a small bowl. Bring remaining juice and all other ingredients to a boil in saucepan. Add softened gelatin; stir until dissolved. Pour mixture into one large or four individual molds which have been sprayed with nonstick cooking spray; refrigerate until firm. Loosen around the edges; unmold on crisp greens and serve with Miracle Whip or similar creamy salad dressing thinned slightly with tomato juice.

Hints and Helps
   This aspic is even better with up to 1 cup diced celery and/or up to 1/2 cup sliced pimiento olives added just before pouring into molds.

BEET ASPIC

1 1-lb. can beets, julienne or diced
Beet juice drained from canned beets plus enough
  water to make 2-1/2 cups
1 12-oz. can vegetable juice cocktail
2 envelopes unflavored gelatin
2 finely sliced green onions, including tops
4 TBS. lemon juice
2 TBS. brown sugar
1 tsp. Worcestershire sauce
4 drops Tabasco
1 cup celery, diced

Prepare 4 cups of liquid; soften gelatin in 1 cup of the liquid. Pour remaining 3 cups of liquid into saucepan and add all other ingredients, except beets and celery. Bring to a boil; add gelatin, stirring until dissolved. Let cool slightly; stir in beets and celery. Chill until partially set. Stir to mix, then ladle into one large or several small individual molds which have been sprayed with nonstick cooking spray. Refrigerate until firm. Loosen around edges, unmold on crisp greens and serve with Miracle Whip or similar creamy salad dressing thinned slightly with lemon juice.

BEVERAGES AND BOOZE

INSTANT COFFEE

If the taste of instant coffee powder or crystals leaves you unimpressed, here's The Real Thing, but instantly available!

1 part ground coffee
4 parts water

Combine coffee and water and let sit at least 6 to 8 hours, stirring occasionally. Pour through a coffee filter placed in a strainer or colander and store in refrigerator in container with lid.

For each cup of coffee, spoon 2 to 3 table-spoons (or to taste) Instant Coffee in a cup and add extremely hot or boiling water.

For iced coffee, cold water and ice cubes can be substituted for the hot.

Hints and Helps
Coffee hates metal, so use glass or plastic containers for preparation and storage. Also, stir with wooden spoon or rubber spatula.

In preparing, water of any temperature can be used, but I prefer to heat fresh water to boiling, let cool for a few minutes, then pour over the grounds. I like to think it maximizes the flavor.

SPICED COFFEE MIX

1 cup instant coffee crystals or powder
1 cup granulated sugar
1 TBS. All-purpose Baking Spice (see recipe)
   OR 1 TBS. ground cinnamon
3 tsp. Dried Orange Peel (see recipe)

Thoroughly combine all ingredients (they will never blend completely) and store in container with tight-fitting lid. To serve, place 2 rounded teaspoons (or to taste) of mix in a mug and add freshly boiled water, stirring to dissolve.

Variation
One cup of brown sugar or a combination of brown and granulated sugars can be substituted for the 1 cup of granulated sugar specified above. This brown sugar coffee mix may eventually become somewhat gummy; however, this will not affect the flavor.

COFFEE VIENNA MIX

2/3 cup granulated sugar
2/3 cup instant nonfat dry milk solids
1/2 cup instant coffee crystals or powder
1 tsp. All-purpose Baking Spice (see recipe)
    OR 1 tsp. ground cinnamon

Combine all ingredients and store in container with tight-fitting lid. To serve, place 2 rounded teaspoons (or to taste) of mix in a cup and add freshly boiled water, stirring to dissolve.

Variation
If you prefer freshly brewed coffee, prepare Coffee Vienna Mix omitting the instant coffee crystals or powder. To serve, stir in 1 to 2 rounded teaspoons (or to taste) of coffee-free mix in a cup of hot coffee.

COFFEE SEVILLE MIX

1 cup instant nonfat dry milk solids
3/4 cup granulated sugar
1/2 cup instant coffee crystals or powder
2 tsp. Dried Orange Peel (see recipe)

Combine all ingredients and store in container with tight-fitting lid. To serve, place 2 rounded teaspoons (or to taste) of mix in a cup and add freshly boiled water, stirring to dissolve.

Variation

If you prefer freshly brewed coffee, prepare Coffee Seville Mix omitting the instant coffee crystals or powder. To serve, stir in 1 to 2 rounded teaspoons (or to taste) of coffee-free mix in a cup of hot coffee.

EASY MOCHA MIX

1 cup instant nonfat dry milk solids
1/2 cup granulated sugar
1/2 cup instant coffee powder or crystals
2 TBS. unsweetened cocoa

Combine all ingredients and store in container with tight-fitting lid. To serve, place 2 rounded teaspoons (or to taste) of mix in a cup and add freshly boiled water, stirring to dissolve.

Variation
If you prefer freshly brewed coffee, prepare Easy Mocha Mix omitting the instant coffee powder or crystals. To serve, stir in 1 to 2 rounded teaspoons (or to taste) of coffee-free mix in a cup of hot coffee.

SPICY MOCHA MIX

1 cup instant nonfat dry milk solids
1 cup granulated sugar
1/2 cup nondairy creamer powder
1/2 cup unsweetened cocoa
3 TBS. instant coffee powder or crystals
3/4 tsp. All-purpose Baking Spice (see recipe)
    OR 1/2 tsp. ground allspice and 1/4 tsp.
    ground cinnamon
1/4 tsp. salt

Combine all ingredients in a bowl. Store in container with tight-fitting lid. To serve, spoon 3 tablespoons (or to taste) Spicy Mocha Mix in a mug; add 3/4 cup of boiling water; stir until dissolved. If desired, top with miniature marshmallows.

HOT COCOA MIX

2 cups instant nonfat dry milk solids
3/4 cup granulated sugar
1/2 cup unsweetened cocoa
1/2 tsp. salt

Combine all ingredients thoroughly and store in covered container. To serve, spoon 2 heaping tablespoons (or to taste) of mix into mug and stir in freshly boiled water. Add 1/2 teaspoon Vanilla Extract (see recipe) for smoother flavor, if desired.

Hints and Helps

For SUGAR-FREE HOT COCOA MIX, substitute 3/4 cup of powdered low-calorie sugar replacement for the 3/4 cup granulated sugar.

SPICED TEA MIX

This is sometimes called "Russian" Tea, but Russian, it ain't. And, while loaded with sugar, it is the world's greatest pick-me-up on a cold, rainy day.

3/4 cup instant powdered tea
1 cup powdered orange-flavor breakfast drink
1/2 cup powdered lemonade mix
1/3 to 1/2 cup granulated sugar
1-1/2 tsp. All-Purpose Baking Spice (see recipe)
    OR 1 tsp. ground cinnamon and 1 tsp. ground
    nutmeg

Combine all ingredients as thoroughly as possible (they will never blend completely) and store in covered container. To serve, spoon 2 to 3 heaping teaspoons (or to taste) in a cup and add freshly boiled water, stirring to dissolve.

LEMONADE MIX

If you live in the West, you may frequently be blessed (or burdened) with a largess of free lemons. That is the time to take full advantage of the saying "When stuck with a lemon, make lemonade."

> 1 cup water
> Rind of 2 lemons cut in thin strips
> 2 cups granulated sugar
> 1/4 tsp. salt
> 1-1/2 to 2-1/2 cups of lemon juice, depending
>   upon tartness of lemons

Gently boil all ingredients, except lemon juice, for 5 minutes. Cool slightly and add juice; strain, store in covered container in refrigerator, or freeze (mix will become a slush, easy to spoon without thawing).

To serve, stir 2 tablespoons (or to taste) of mix into glass; add cold water and ice cubes. Or, for hot beverage, combine in mug with freshly boiled water.

ORANGE JULIUS

1 6-oz. can frozen orange juice concentrate
1 cup cold water
1 cup milk
1/2 cup granulated sugar
1 tsp. Vanilla Extract (see recipe)
5 to 6 ice cubes

Combine all ingredients in a blender and blend approximately 30 seconds.

DRAMBUIE

2 cups granulated sugar
1 cup water
2 cups Scotch whiskey
1/2 tsp. anise extract
1/4 tsp. Vanilla Extract (see recipe)

Combine sugar and water in a saucepan and bring to a boil; simmer for 5 minutes, stirring occasionally. Cool slightly; add Scotch whiskey, anise extract, and Vanilla Extract. Pour into quart bottle and cap tightly. Before serving, age for 10 days, lightly shaking bottle occasionally.

AMARETTO

When concocting this liqueur, use house brands of everything, except the water!

    2 cups granulated sugar
    2 cups water
    2 cups brandy
    2 cups vodka
    4 tsp. almond extract

Combine sugar and water in a large saucepan; bring to boiling. Reduce heat and simmer, uncovered, for 10 minutes, stirring occasionally. Remove from heat; cool slightly. Stir in remaining ingredients. Store in jars with lids or stoppered decanter.

KAHLÚA

If you use house brands of sugar, coffee, and bourbon in this home-brew, it won't hurt so much when you check the price of a single vanilla bean (be sure to buy it at your bulk food store).

3-1/2 cups granulated sugar
3 cups water
1 cup instant coffee crystals or powder
1 fifth bourbon (3 cups)
1 vanilla bean

Combine sugar with 2 cups of the water in a large saucepan and bring to a boil, stirring until sugar dissolves completely . Set aside to cool. Bring remaining 1 cup of water to boil and mix with coffee; let stand until cool. Chop vanilla bean fine and place in a half-gallon bottle. Funnel sugar mixture and coffee mixture into the bottle. Add the bourbon and cap tightly. Place the bottle in a conspicuous spot (so you won't forget it) and shake vigorously once a day for *three weeks*! Strain into a half-gallon bottle with tight-fitting cap.

GALLIANO

Save by using house brands of every ingredient you can.

6 cups granulated sugar
5 cups water
1/2 tsp. orange extract
1/2 tsp. anise extract
1/8 tsp. almond extract
2 or 3 drops yellow food color
1 quart vodka

Combine sugar and water in a large saucepan and boil 5 minutes stirring occasionally. Cool to room temperature and add all remaining ingredients, adding vodka last. Makes about 2-3/4 quarts.

BAILEY'S IRISH CREAM

14 oz. whipping cream
10 oz. Sweetened Condensed milk (see recipe)
2 eggs
1 TBS. instant coffee powder or crystals
1 cup Irish whiskey, or to taste

Using a whisk or electric mixer, combine all ingredients until thoroughly blended. (If using coffee crystals, they may not dissolve immediately. Let mixture rest for 10 minutes or more and blend again.) Refrigerate in container with tight-fitting lid; will keep up to one month or more.

Variations
Substitute the following for the Irish whiskey:
Scotch Cream — use Scotch whiskey
Cuban Cream — use rum
American Cream — use bourbon whiskey
French Cream — use brandy

SIMPLE SUBSTITUTES

SIMPLE SUBSTITUTES
(Missing a little something?)

Arrowroot (for thickening) — 1-3/4 TBS. flour for each 2 tsp. arrowroot.

Baking powder — replace 1/2 cup liquid with 1/4 tsp. baking soda plus 1/2 cup sour milk.

Butter (in cooking or baking) — 7/8 cup vegetable oil for each 1 cup butter OR 1 cup shortening plus 1/2 tsp. salt.

Cornstarch (for thickening) — 2 TBS. all-purpose flour for each 1 TBS. cornstarch OR 4 tsp. quick-cooking tapioca.

Cream, sour, heavy (in cooking and baking) — 1/3 cup margarine plus 2/3 cup milk for each 1 cup heavy sour cream.

Cream, sour, heavy (for dips and garnishes) — 1 cup low-fat cottage cheese, 1 TBS. lemon juice, 1 TBS. milk, blended until smooth for each 1 cup of heavy sour cream.

Cream (to sour) — add 1-1/3 TBS. vinegar OR 1-1/2 TBS. lemon juice to 1 cup cream. Let stand for 5 minutes.

Egg yolks (in custard) — 1 whole egg for each 2 egg yolks.

Flour, cake, sifted — 7/8 cup all-purpose flour, sifted (1 cup less 2 TBS.) for each 1 cup of sifted cake flour.

Herbs — 1 tsp. dried herbs for each 1 TBS. fresh herbs.

Honey — substitute molasses, cup for cup.

Lemon juice (in cooking, salad dressings) — in most cases, vinegar may be substituted, in equal portions.

Margarine (in cooking and baking) — 7/8 cup vegetable oil for each 1 cup margarine OR 1 cup shortening plus 1/2 tsp. salt.

Milk, whole (in cooking and baking) — 1/2 cup evaporated milk and 1/2 cup water for each 1 cup of milk OR 1 cup reconstituted nonfat dry milk plus 2 tsp. margarine.

Milk, sweet — 1 cup of sour milk plus 1/2 tsp. baking soda for each cup of sweet milk.

Milk, sour or buttermilk — add 1-1/3 TBS. vinegar OR 1-1/2 TBS. lemon juice to 1 cup sweet milk. Let stand 5 minutes.

Molasses — substitute honey, cup for cup.

Mustard, dry — 1 TBS. prepared mustard for each 1 tsp. dry mustard.

Onion, fresh — 1 TBS. minced dried onion, rehydrated, for each 1 small fresh onion.

Sugar, granulated (in baking) — 1 cup molasses plus 1/2 tsp. baking soda for each 1 cup of sugar. Reduce liquid by 1/4 cup.

— 1 cup honey plus plus 1/2 tsp. baking soda for each 1 cup of sugar. Reduce the liquid by 1/4 cup.

— 1 cup maple syrup plus 1/4 cup light corn syrup for each 1 cup of sugar. Reduce the liquid by 1/4 cup.

Tomato catsup or chili sauce (in cooking) — 1 cup tomato sauce plus 1/2 cup sugar and 2 TBS. vinegar for each 1 cup catsup or chili sauce.

Tomato juice — 1/2 cup tomato sauce plus 1/2 cup water for each 1 cup tomato juice.

THE VERY END

WORLD'S DAMNEDEST RECIPE

Does this recipe belong in this book? Or, any other? NO! But I dare you to try it. It works!

Soda crackers (saltines)
Margarine
Seasoned Salt (see recipe) or salt

Preheat oven to 450°. Melt margarine. Soak crackers in ice water for exactly 8 minutes. Remove with slotted spatula onto cookie sheet. Dot them with melted margarine and sprinkle very, very lightly with Seasoned Salt. Bake approximately 12 minutes until crackers are slightly puffed and light brown. Serve with soups or spreads.

INDEX

INDEX

ABOUT THE AUTHOR

According to Ben Howard, he was born in the latter part of the Dark Ages, when everyone's television ran on kerosene. He was one of twins born in a brand new hospital in Keene, New Hampshire, which was cause for some celebration. However, when the twosome proved to be fraternal (vs. identical), the hospital put away the confetti.

His formative years were spent in Valparaiso, Indiana, where being the middle of five children, he learned to claw his way either up or down to get his share. Howard spent three and one-half years in the U.S. Navy during WW II. As Supply and Disbursing Officer for a destroyer escort, he was responsible for purchasing all foodstuffs and planning all menus for the ship's staff. There are no reports of any personnel ever fainting from malnutrition; however, the crew never understood why he ordered Cheddar cheese slices served with apple pie.

Graduating from Indiana University, Howard entered the advertising racket as copywriter, then account executive, and for nearly 40 years bamboozled the Great American Public into buying products ranging from soda crackers to snake-bite kits.

Howard currently lives in Fairfax, California, and is not quite sure whether he is retired or just retarded. He claims to have cooked for himself — and sometimes others — for a good part of his life, that no one ever died, and that he is still vertical.

He sincerely hopes you enjoy his book.

TO ORDER

For additional copies of *Make Your Own Mixes*, telephone TOLL FREE 1-800-356-9315 or FAX TOLL FREE 1-800-242-0046. MasterCard/VISA accepted. To order *Make Your Own Mixes* directly from the publisher, send your check or money order for $14.95 plus $3.00 shipping and handling ($17.95 postpaid) to:

Rainbow Books, Inc.,
Order Dept. 1-T,
P.O. Box 430,
Highland City, FL 33846-0430.

For QUANTITY PURCHASES, telephone Rainbow Books, Inc., 1-813-648-4420 or write to Rainbow Books, Inc., P.O. Box 430, Highland City, FL 33846-0430.